IMAGES
of America

Lighthouses of Humboldt County

On the Cover: Trinidad Head Lighthouse has been in operation since 1871. After 145 years in operation, the US Coast Guard relinquished the 12 acres on Trinidad Head where the lighthouse resides to the Bureau of Land Management (BLM) in 2014. The BLM, the City of Trinidad, the Trinidad Rancheria, and the Yurok tribe cooperatively developed the management plan allowing for public access to the site. The US Coast Guard continues to operate the navigational beacon with a fiber optic lens. The BLM partners with Trinidad Museum Society docents who lead lighthouse tours on the first Saturday of every month. (Humboldt County Collection, Humboldt State University.)

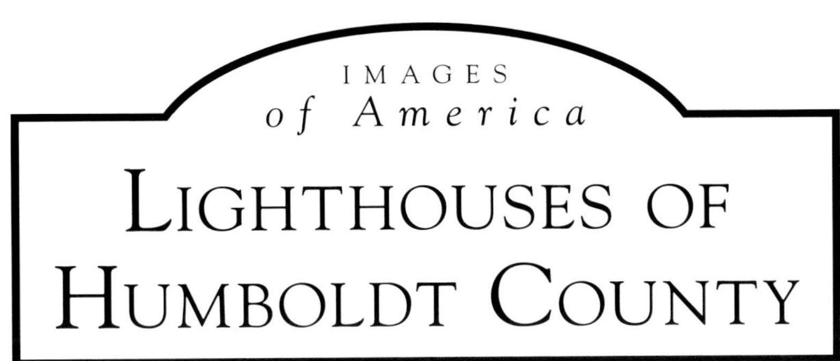

Julie Clark
Foreword by Jon Humboldt Gates

ISBN 978-1-4671-0758-7

Published by Arcadia Publishing
Charleston, South Carolina

Printed in the United States of America

Library of Congress Control Number: 2021941795

For all general information, please contact Arcadia Publishing:
Telephone 843-853-2070
Fax 843-853-0044
E-mail sales@arcadiapublishing.com
For customer service and orders:
Toll-Free 1-888-313-2665

Visit us on the Internet at www.arcadiapublishing.com

This book is dedicated to the Trinidad Museum Society and the Trinidad Rancheria, whose partnerships are invaluable; and to the Tsurai, the first people on the land, whose descendants continue to view Trinidad Head as a culturally and spiritually significant place.

Contents

Foreword

For more than a century, lighthouses along the Humboldt County coast have served as beacons for generations of my family. My great-grandparents arrived in Humboldt Bay by ship in the late 1800s when some of the early lighthouses were being constructed. At the turn of the century, my grandparents sailed aboard the steamships *Pomona* and *Corona*, traveling the coast to San Francisco and the Klondike. From the decks of those ships, they could see the lighthouses of Punta Gorda, Cape Mendocino, Trinidad Head, and Humboldt Bay.

My father commercially fished these coastal waters and reefs beginning in the 1940s after serving in the US Navy and Merchant Marine. He later ran the Humboldt Bar pilot boat. I went to sea with him many times. Seeing the Blunts Reef Light Ship off Cape Mendocino in the 1960s remains a stark, vivid memory of that lone ship and stoic crew, anchored around the clock in some of the roughest waters on the California coast.

Over the years, I walked the entire Humboldt County coastline, visiting the isolated ruins of the Punta Gorda and Cape Mendocino lighthouses. I lived in Trinidad for 20 years and often hiked to the point above the lighthouse. But Cape Mendocino was the most primal environment. It was isolated, wild, and off limits. I would discreetly hike to the dilapidated structure at the edge of a cliff and climb a rusty ladder into the glassed beacon tower. It teetered over 440 feet above the ocean. In those solitary moments, I would find inspiration and imagine the days when the lighthouse was operational and the rugged lifestyles of those who lived there, and I would enjoy the enormous Pacific panoramas.

—Jon Humboldt Gates

Acknowledgments

This project is a direct result of the support I receive from the Bureau of Land Management, Arcata Field Office. Without that office's trust, confidence, and support, this book would just be an idea. The thoughtful, interested community of Humboldt County makes for a compelling audience; they will find joy in reading about its lighthouses and visit the public lands where these beacons once stood. Special thanks to Humboldt State University professor and mentor in history, Gayle Olson-Raymer, who has not only influenced my life but also thousands of others in their pursuit of the truth about our collective history. Thanks to my husband, Cris, who is my beacon of light. Many thanks to the Trinidad Museum Society and Patti Fleschner, who provided me with photographs, stories, and heartfelt memories to bring the past alive.

Image Credits Key

BLM: Bureau of Land Management
HCC: Humboldt County Collection, Humboldt State University
HCHS: Humboldt County Historical Society
MVHS: Mattole Valley Historical Society
USCG: US Coast Guard
USLHS: US Lighthouse Society

INTRODUCTION

The Pacific Northwest coast is one of the most windswept areas in the world. Cold Pacific currents, powerful Alaskan winter storms, towering offshore rocks, fog, and dangerous harbor entrance bars consistently threatened sailing vessels that come near the impenetrable coast. Since the 1500s, seafaring explorers began searching for viable ports and natural harbors along the rugged northern California coast. But it was not until 1806 that an American-Russian fur trading vessel under the command of Jonathon Winship entered what he referred to as a "spacious sound"—Humboldt Bay. The crew, however, failed to map it, and Humboldt Bay remained hidden and merely a rumor until 1849, when it was discovered by an overland party led by gold merchant Josiah Gregg from Weaverville. Once the party found the harbor, the Wiyot chief Ki-we-lat-tah gave the hungry explorers clams before they embarked south to San Francisco to tell the news of their discovery. Little did the chief know, the future of Humboldt Bay, their native culture, and the surrounding area would be altered forever.

Thereafter, the race for north coast settlement began in earnest. In the spring of 1850, Capt. Hans Buhne piloted the schooner *Laura Virginia* into Humboldt Bay, making him the first captain to bring a ship across the bar. The new community of Eureka was established, based upon the lucrative "redwood gold" that relied heavily on ships for export and import. The bay, however, resembled a lagoon and the width and depth of the entrance varied tremendously, which caused delays in shipping. The entrance was also dangerous. Between 1853 and 1881, eighty-one people drowned coming through the narrow bar passage. The expanding population and the exportation of unique resources such as redwoods, mining supplies, and fisheries were dependent on safe harbors and the illumination of the coast. The need for lighthouses on the California seaboard became critical for its economic success.

In 1852, the US Lighthouse Board was created, and the US Department of the Treasury allocated $148,000 to build 16 lighthouses along the western seaboard. California locations included Alcatraz Island, Fort Point, Point Bonita, Point Pinos, the Farallon Islands, Point Loma, Santa Barbara, Point Conception, Humboldt Harbor, and Crescent City; the Oregon location was the entrance to the Umpqua River, Cape Disappointment; and Washington locations included Cape Flattery, New Dungeness, Smith Island, and Wilapa Bay. Coast surveyor Alexander D. Bache, grandson of Benjamin Franklin, was responsible for surveying the locations. While Bache's crew performed tests and checked for easy access and suitable locations along the shoreline, they had little understanding of the weather patterns and the severity of the Pacific Coast conditions. This lack of understanding ensured that Humboldt's first lighthouse would have a rocky start, and it was doomed from its conception.

The Humboldt Harbor Lighthouse (1855), built in what is now the Samoa Dunes National Recreation Area, was designed with lighthouse keeper's quarters and a rising tower through the center of the structure. The light, a fourth-order Fresnel lens, could be seen by ship captains for

20 nautical miles. However, due to its poor location in the sand dunes—the tower's light was a mere 50 feet above mean tide—the lack of water, constant fog, and the high turnover rate of lighthouse keepers, it was all but abandoned and left to deteriorate in favor of a new light at Table Bluff in 1892.

Dangerous coastal geography and conditions influenced the need for and immediate growth of lighthouses. Between 1850 and 1865, there were 25 wrecks and hundreds of drownings, including one of the most infamous wrecks in maritime history, the *Brother Jonathan*. In 1865, the *Brother Jonathan*, carrying 200 passengers from San Francisco to Portland, collided with St. George Reef near Crescent City, and 161 people drowned. This catastrophe, along with others, spurred funding and the need for additional lighthouses in Humboldt County, starting with Cape Mendocino (established 1868), Trinidad Head (established 1871), Table Bluff (established 1892), and Punta Gorda (established 1911). These were not just lighthouses but also lighthouse stations, equipped with a Fresnel lens, fog signal building, lighthouse keeper dwellings, support structures such as barns, and most importantly, a lighthouse keeper and their assistants.

Lighthouse keeping was not only a vocation but also a lifestyle and one that required appointment. It was restricted to persons between the ages of 18 and 50 who could read, write, and keep accounts. They were required to perform manual labor, pull and sail a boat, do minor repairs, and keep structures painted, whitewashed, and in working order. Most lighthouse keepers did not have nautical backgrounds but simply came for rewarding physical work. Theirs was a career that often spanned multiple generations with intermarriage between keepers and their families. By the 1950s, with advancing technology, lights became automated and keeping them became obsolete.

In the 1950s, when lighthouse technology shifted to automation, there was no longer a need for lighthouse keepers and many of the lighthouses they once occupied. Today, the only operational Humboldt County lighthouse is in Trinidad. The remaining four lighthouse sites, all of which are maintained by the Bureau of Land Management (BLM), are located on public land and are part of the National Conservation Lands, California Coastal National Monument (CCNM), and King Range National Conservation Area. As public stewards of these lighthouses, the BLM conserves a piece of American history by providing public tours and creating historical interpretive panels and living history demonstrations that reflect on how maritime traffic was once the lifeblood of Humboldt County and the rest of the world. Visitors are encouraged to explore these public lands where lighthouses played such an integral part in California's history.

One

Rocky Beginnings

The Humboldt County coastline has been described as one of the most dangerous and volatile shores in the world. Navigating sailing vessels into the coastal harbors has been historically difficult since 16th-century European exploration. For centuries, Spanish galleons sailed north and south without seeing a viable entrance into the well-hidden Humboldt Bay. Shortly after California became a state in 1850, Humboldt Bay was "discovered," and the inevitable settlement around the bay was immediate. Instead of gold mining commerce, the redwoods became the primary economic commodity, and "redwood gold" topped exportation. The land immediately around the bay saw the development of Eureka and Union Town, presently Arcata. By 1860, indigenous Wiyot people found themselves displaced from their homeland of thousands of years and forced to rancherias and land that was of no interest to businessmen or settlers. Early merchants like Capt. Hans Buhne shifted their goals of becoming gold merchants to the business of supporting the import and exportation of redwood and fisheries. In the period between 1853 and 1880, eighty-one people, including Buhne's wife, Mary, were killed while navigating their vessels across the Humboldt Bar. It was years before the most dangerous entrance in the world was fortified with jetties, the Humboldt Harbor Lighthouse, and the establishment of a lifesaving station. Between 1850 and 1975, one hundred and twenty shipwrecks along the Humboldt–Del Norte Coast prompted continuous funding of lighthouses and jetty improvements. The most infamous shipwrecks, the *Brother Jonathon* near Crescent City in 1865 and the USS *Milwaukee Samoa* disaster in 1917, led to continuous federal funding through the US Department of the Treasury and US Army Corps of Engineers to fortify the jetties and fund the lighthouses. Humboldt County's economic historic and present viability depends on sound jetties, a safe entrance into Humboldt Bay, and lights to illuminate its coast.

For two and a half centuries, from 1565 to 1815, Spanish galleons took the yearly route from Manila, Philippines, to Acapulco, Mexico, carrying large amounts of silver coin, china, spices, gold, etc. They skirted the rugged coast from Cape Mendocino to the tip of Baja California but avoided getting too close to the shore because of the dense fog that hid the reefs and rocks just underneath the surface. Two galleons—the *Espiritu Santo* and the *Jesus Maria*—narrowly escaped a shipwreck at Cape Mendocino. During the history of this route, 30 ships were lost and over 60 million pesos, china, precious metal, and gems all went missing. Legend claims that a galleon wrecked on the rugged coast and its treasure was stashed away in a cave near King Peak. Years later, an earthquake sealed that cave forever. (Above, courtesy of Huntington Library; below, courtesy of University of Southern California.)

The impact of white settlers on Native American tribes was beyond devastating. Their resources, their homeland, and their way of life were forever altered and displaced. Over time, the relationship between the two cultures led to violence and ultimately genocide. In 1870, a Eureka newspaper journalist interviewed Captain John, Te-nas-te-nah, in Hoopa. Born at the lower Mad River, he recounted that on the morning of his birth, a ship of palefaces touched the shore and gave the tribes knives, beads, and paint. They wore strange clothes and garments, and the tribe greeted the explorers with mixed excitement and wonder. But others saw it as a beginning to an end with degradation and despair for the future of their tribe. (Above, courtesy of Carlton Watkins; right, courtesy of Palmquist Collection, Humboldt State University.)

In November 1849, a group of eight gold merchants known as the Gregg party left Weaverville in search of a rumored Trinity Bay, supposedly west of Weaverville about 100 miles. They needed an easier way to supply the gold miners in the Trinity mountains. The group packed 10 days of food, but that eventually turned into 40 days of walking and nearly starving when they finally reached the coast. Among these men were David A. Buck, Josiah Gregg, and Lewis Keyser Wood. According to Wood's journals, once they arrived on the coast, they walked down from present-day Mad River, followed the beach, and camped. It was there that they took a sip of the lagoon water and realized they were drinking from Humboldt Bay. (Left, courtesy of Maurice Fulton; below, courtesy of Palmquist Collection, Humboldt State University.)

Much of the Gregg party details of finding Humboldt Bay were journaled by Lewis Keyser Wood. He described camping on Christmas day near the site of the present-day Crabs Baseball Field in Arcata. The following day, they encountered an Indian by the name of Ki-we-lat-tah, a Wiyot chief who supplied the party with clams. The explorers journeyed south to San Francisco to tell others of their discovery but not without strife. Josiah Gregg died along the way, and L.K. Wood and the rest of the party fought off grizzly bears near the site of Bear Butte, north of Redway. L.K. Wood eventually settled in Arcata where he became the county clerk and built a house on his farm called Ki-we-lat-tah. (Right, courtesy of HCC; below, courtesy of Palmquist Collection, Humboldt State University.)

Hans Buhne, born in Denmark in 1822, left home at 16, became a sailor, and journeyed around the world by boat. He survived shipwrecks, whaled around Russia, and landed in San Francisco in 1850 broke and tenacious for more adventures. He was selected as second mate on the *Laura Virginia*, the first vessel to sail into Humboldt Bay. Little did Buhne know that he would be the first one to pilot the ship across the perilous Humboldt Bar. Captain Buhne selected the red bluff directly east that would eventually become home and a trading and supply city for the Trinity mines. The crew built makeshift shacks, developed a city plat, and named it Humboldt City after the prominent German naturalist Alexander Von Humboldt. By 1852, the coastal survey was complete, and Bucksport, Eureka, and Union Town (now Arcata) were viable towns on the map. (Left, courtesy of HCC; below, courtesy of US Coastal Survey.)

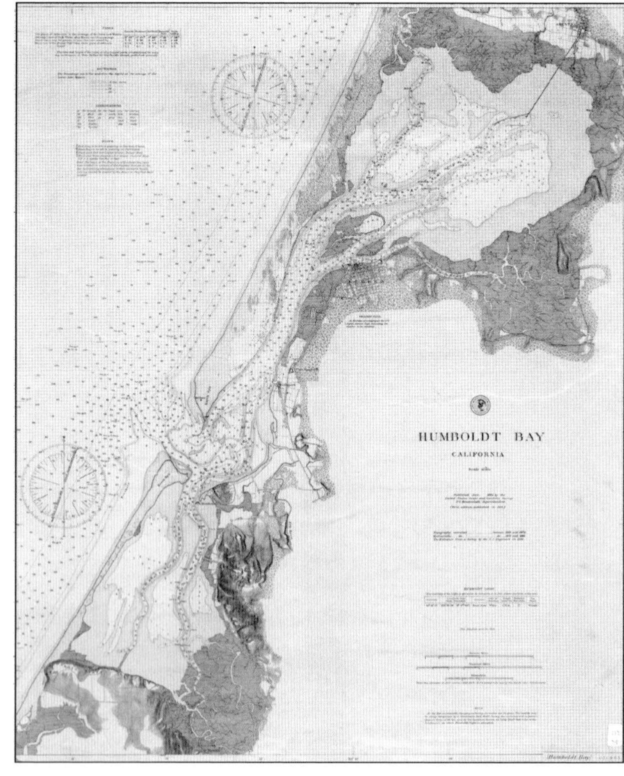

Before the north and south jetties were constructed, navigating into Humboldt Bay was nearly impossible. In the 1850s, the Humboldt Bar was identified as the most dangerous and hazardous in California. To mitigate the unpredictable entrance and exit of Humboldt Bay, a competent bar pilot with tugboat experience was needed. It was not until 1852 with the wreck of the redwood cargo ship *Home*, Ryan and Duff Lumber Company owners invested in a steam tugboat and made Capt. Hans Buhne their official bar pilot. The steam tug *Mary Ann* was the queen of tugs that operated in and out of Humboldt Bay for 40 years. During *Mary Ann*'s tenure, shipwrecks decreased dramatically. However, Humboldt Bay was in dire need of jetties. (Both, courtesy of HCC Collection, Humboldt State University.)

INDEPENDENT LINE
FOR
CALIFORNIA,
Opposition to the Old Monopoly
AT REDUCED RATES OF FARE,

The new and Splendid Steamship
Brother Jonathan
1800 Tons Burthen,
With accommodations for 700 Passengers, and unrivalled speed, having been thoroughly overhauled, enlarged, strengthened and improved,
Will sail for Chagres and San Juan
On Thursday, Feb. 26, at 3 P.M.,
FROM PIER 4, N. R
For Freight or Passage, at REDUCED rates, apply to
E MILLS, Agent,
51 Cortlandt street.

Labeled the worst maritime disaster in maritime history, the *Brother Jonathon* sank close to St. George Reef near Crescent City on July 30, 1865, and among the 219 passengers, 200 people drowned. The ship was carrying military supplies and animals, heavy mining and railroad equipment, and an Army payroll in newly minted gold coin. The steam-driven side-wheeler had left San Francisco and was traveling to Vancouver with a stop in Portland. Gale force winds caused the ship to collide with the jagged rocks near St. George Reef, and the ship sank in less than 30 minutes. Among the passengers was Brig. Gen. George Wright, the Union commander of the Department of the Pacific. This tragic event, along with the many shipwrecks on the north coast of California, contributed to the funding of additional lighthouses in the Pacific Northwest. (Above, courtesy of Mike and Carol McKinney; left, courtesy of Del Norte County Historical Society.)

The *Northerner* mail and passenger steam ship was one of many that traveled from San Francisco north to Portland and on to Canada. In the steam ship era, this was the fastest route, traveling 10 to 12 miles per hour. The *Northerner* left on January 4, 1860, and by 5:00 p.m. the next day, four miles from Cape Mendocino, the ship struck a rock no bigger "than a man's head" near Blunts Reef. Capt. W.L. Dall headed for the shores near Centerville Beach, just west of Ferndale. While the ship was sinking, Captain Dall handed his favorite cabin boy $500, but when the boy boarded a lifeboat with the captain, Dall told him to give back the money. The cabin boy refused and found himself $500 richer as well as a survivor, who swam to nearby Centerville Beach. In 1921, a cross was placed on the bluff overlooking the beach in memorial of the 38 drowning victims. Fourteen of them were temporarily buried on shore while the rest were lost at sea. (Right, courtesy of *Daily Alta*; below, courtesy of Ellin Beltz.)

UNITED STATES MAIL LINE

FOR

PORTLAND,

Victoria, Port Townsend and Olympia.

The Mail Steamship

NORTHERNER,

W. L. DALL..COMMANDER,

Will leave Folsom street wharf

For the Above Port

on

TUESDAY,..........................JAN. 3, 1860,

At 4 o'clock P. M.

FORBES & BABCOCK, Agents.

For Freight or Passage, apply on board, or to the Agents of the Pacific Mail Steamship Company, corner Sacramento and Leidesdorff streets.

Bills of lading will be furnished by the Purser to shippers of cargo. None others than those so furnished will be received.

On June 11, 1906, the *Corinthian*, bound for San Francisco, crossed Humboldt Bar and attempted to navigate through the south channel. Instead, the ship encountered a huge wave, causing her to take on water and ultimately wreck a mile above the Humboldt Bay entrance. One of the two fatalities was Thomas McCormick, a graduate of St. Ignatius in San Francisco. McCormick had been shanghaied and smuggled aboard the *North Fork* ship in San Francisco. He was promised voyage to China but instead found himself lied to and in Eureka. Once he arrived, he telegrammed his parents, told them what had happened, and boarded a return trip on the *Corinthian* as a cook's helper. He was in the galley when a wave struck the vessel, and he was carried overboard. This wreck was one of many that prompted constant work and funding on the north and south jetties. (Both, courtesy of HCHS.)

On March 1, 1907, the steamer *Corona* was considered the best steam ship service between Eureka and San Francisco until it wrecked on the Humboldt Bar with 100 passengers aboard. The boat was attempting to go into port when strong wind pushed it onto the north jetty. The quartermaster lowered a rescue boat to go to shore, but two of the sailors drowned when that boat capsized. The night salon watchman, formerly a marine in the US Navy, stripped to the waist and attempted to carry a line ashore but lost the line in the frigid water when he was ultimately rescued. Multiple unsuccessful attempts at shooting a line were made, but it was the brave crew pilot who picked up the line and brought it ashore. The rescue took six hours while thousands of onlookers came to the beach to watch. Remnants of the *Corona* cofferdam can be seen on the north spit at low tide. (Both, courtesy of HCHS.)

The biggest disaster of Humboldt maritime history occurred in December 1916. Residents of Samoa came out of their houses to see a naval submarine named H3 in distress; it was beached and in the sand. The submariners were trapped inside for over 10 hours when the crew was finally rescued by the Coast Guard Humboldt Life Saving Station via breeches buoy. How did the submarine find itself on the north coast and in this unfortunate event? The US Navy was increasing its presence on the West Coast due to Germany's increase in U-boats. The H3 was running on electric motors in the fog, and with the minimal visibility, it beached. A month later, the US Navy brought in the USS *Milwaukee* to tow the submarine out. (Both, courtesy of US Naval and Heritage Command.)

In January 1917, one month after the submarine H3 was beached, the US Navy was intent on towing the submarine safely off the shore. It brought in the USS *Milwaukee*, a 10,000-ton, 426-foot-long, 66-foot-wide ship commanded by Lt. W.F. Newton. The plan was to attach a line to the submarine while the USS *Iroquois* and the USS *Cheyenne* anchored the heavy ship into place. Hundreds of onlookers came down to the beach to witness the *Milwaukee*'s attempt to pull the submarine that had, by this time, sunk over six feet in the sand. Once the *Milwaukee* started to pull the sunken submarine, it had a vacuum effect, and the *Milwaukee* hit the bottom of the shore, filled with water, flooded her engine room, and was carried into the breakers. The Navy now had to salvage what was left of the $7 million ship and contract out the submarine tow. (Both, courtesy of US Naval History and Heritage Command.)

Humboldt County has always been known for its people who roll up their sleeves and do the impossible, and the engineering firm Mercer Frasier was no exception. It was able to rescue the H3 submarine out of the sand when the US Navy's efforts failed. An out-of-the-area firm bid the job at $150,000, while the local Mercer Frasier did it for $18,000. Mercer Frasier hoisted the sub out of the sand, put it on log rollers, transported H3 down the north spit, and lowered it into Humboldt Bay. H3 was then returned to San Pedro, California, where she served as flagship of Submarine Division 7, participating in exercises and operations along the coast until 1922. She was decommissioned and scrapped by the Navy in 1931. (Both, courtesy of US Naval History and Heritage Command.)

One can see the ghost of the *Milwaukee* with a row of bulkheads peeking over the low tide more than 100 years later. Two thirds of the vessel is still there, but it is buried in the dense sand. The *Milwaukee* survived mostly intact until 1943, when valuable metal for the war effort was salvaged. After the USS *Milwaukee* was decommissioned on March 6, 1917, a storm in November 1918 broke the ship in two. Her name was struck from the Naval Vessel Register on June 23, 1919, and her hulk was sold on August 5, 1919. Pictured is the wrecked cruiser's starboard bridge on April 29, 1919, more than two years after she went aground at Samoa. A pier was built and used by salvagers to remove guns and equipment from the ship. (Both, courtesy of US Naval History and Heritage Command.)

The *Roanoke* steamer carried passengers and cargo into Humboldt Bay in the early 1900s. Steamers such as the *Roanoke* and the *Scotia* were in constant danger of heavy surf while crossing the Humboldt Bar. In October 1906, the *Roanoke* and the *Scotia* both went aground after a failure in communication. The *Scotia* steamer turned away from the Humboldt Bay entrance due to the rough seas. The captain failed to communicate the sudden decision to the *Roanoke*, and both steamers drifted toward the beach. The Humboldt Bar entrance was and is one of the most dangerous harbors in the world. The north jetty and south jetty have been under constant reconstruction since their conception. In 1915, a trestle was built on the north jetty, and the jetty was reconstructed with a 1,050-ton concrete monolith added to its seaward end. (Both, courtesy of Palmquist Collection, Humboldt State University.)

From the time the *Laura Virginia* entered Humboldt Bay in 1850, the bar entrance has been problematic. Before 1889 and 1891, the entrance looked much like G.J. Denny's depiction in his 1870 painting titled *Entrance into Humboldt Bay*. In the period between 1853 and 1880, eighty-one people were killed while their vessels were navigated unsuccessfully across the large sand bar, which obstructed the harbor's entrance. Residents, such as Eureka newspaper owner William Ayres, urged the US Army Corps of Engineers to fortify the jetties. The south jetty was built first in 1889 and the north spit in 1891. They were built with piled up rocks and brush. The ever-present waves soon destroyed all their hard-earned efforts. (Courtesy of HCHS.)

By late 1891, the south jetty was about 4,000 feet long and the north jetty was 1,500 feet long. The jetties were constructed by dumping rock from railcars on trestles. The rock, composed of pieces up to eight tons in weight, was quarried in Jacoby Creek and Blue Lake. The following excerpt from a 19th-century US Army Corps of Engineers navigation report describes typical sea conditions at the entrance to Humboldt Bay during the winter months: "It has been reported by masters of vessels that no such heavy seas have been encountered elsewhere in the world, unless perhaps south of the Cape of Good Hope or Cape Horn. It was originally believed that no jetties or such construction could possibly withstand the forces brought to bear by waves during storms, so that the improvement was undertaken with great misgiving." (Left, courtesy of HCHS; below, courtesy of Palmquist Collection, Humboldt State University.)

William Ayres came to Humboldt County in 1860 from Massachusetts. He was one of the first newspaper men in Humboldt County and was the owner of the *Democratic Standard* in Eureka. From 1877 to 1884, Ayres devoted his publication to gaining the attention of Congress and the Army Corps of Engineers to realize his vision of Eureka and Humboldt Bay as the commercial center of fishing and lumbering in Northern California. He suggested a jetty system be built like that of the Mississippi River jetties. The lobbying efforts of local citizens, led unofficially by Ayres, culminated in the passage of the Rivers and Harbors Act of 1881, which led to the construction of a channel and a jetty 6,000 feet long extending northwesterly from the south spit. (Right, courtesy of Keystone View Company; below, courtesy of Palmquist Collection, Humboldt State University.)

The Army Corps of Engineers began construction on the south jetty in 1889 and on the north jetty in 1891. By late 1891, the south jetty was about 4,000 feet long, and the north jetty was 1,500 feet long. A makeshift railroad was constructed on the jetties, and railroad cars delivered the heavy rock, fortifying and raising the jetties in a fixed point and thereby making the bar safer for the many ships navigating in and out of Humboldt Bay. Also during this time, the Humboldt Harbor Lighthouse was deemed ineffective, and a new lighthouse was built at Table Bluff. Pictured below are William Vansant and his wife, Lilian Jean, with their daughter Madeline around 1906. Vansant was the grandson of Sarah Johnson, the second lighthouse keeper of the Humboldt Harbor Lighthouse. (Above, courtesy of HCHS; below, courtesy of Palmquist Collection, Humboldt State University.)

With the never-ending pounding waves coupled with continuous navigation, the jetties are in constant state of repair. In 1898, after the Humboldt Harbor Lighthouse was deemed inadequate, beacon lights were placed on the jetties. Shortly after the lights were installed, they were carried away in severe storms. Currently, the jetty has range lights and sound signals with lighted whistle buoys to guide mariners into the bay. To mitigate the erosion of the jetties, Army Corps engineer Orville Magoon in 1971 designed the dolosse after an African goat ankle. These 5,000 dolosse structures, placed on both jetties between 1971 and 1973, are a landmark in engineering. In 1985, the Army Corps strategically placed another 1,000 on the jetties. Currently in 2021, there are plans to reinforce the jetties once again. (Above, courtesy of Palmquist/Yale Collection, Humboldt State University; below, courtesy of Mark McKenna.)

The north and south jetties are maintained by the US Army Corps of Engineers. The surrounding lands of the north and south spit are comanaged by the BLM Arcata Field Office, Humboldt County, and the California Department of Fish and Wildlife. The Wiyot tribe, the California Coastal Conservancy, and the US Fish and Wildlife Service also cooperate in providing public access. The Samoa Dunes Recreation Area, comprised of 300 acres, offers miles of untouched Pacific Ocean views and attracts OHV (off-highway vehicle) enthusiasts, hikers, sports fisherman, and history seekers. The north spit, located at the end of the Samoa peninsula, is a place to explore maritime and World War II history with the many bunkers and the site of the original Humboldt County lighthouse. Access to the lighthouse ruins is located adjacent to Bunker Road along the one-mile wetland trail loop. The lighthouse structure is completely gone, but there are remnants such as bricks, stone steps that once entered the lighthouse residence, and ivy that the lighthouse keepers planted. (Courtesy of Lindsey Abernathy.)

Two

Lighting the Coast

Two years after California became a state, the rise of commerce, transportation, exploration, and shipwrecks generated a need for safe harbors and lighthouses illuminating the Pacific Coast. In 1851, Congress appropriated $158,000 for seven lighthouses in California and three in Oregon. Humboldt County's first light station, the Humboldt Harbor Lighthouse, located in the sand dunes of the north jetty, was predestined to fail from the beginning. From its inception in 1851 to 1856 when the light was finally lit, it faced many roadblocks. Management of lighthouses in the first 50 years of California history was difficult, with changes in government departments, shifts in congressional funding, cutting-edge lighthouse technology, population booms, and increased shipwrecks. All of this led to additional funding appropriations for four more Humboldt County lighthouse stations: Cape Mendocino (1868), Trinidad Head (1871), Table Bluff (1892), and Punta Gorda (1912). Each of these lighthouses had unique characteristics and were aptly nicknamed by their keepers and mariners. Humboldt Harbor and Table Bluff Light Station illuminated "the first important harbor north of San Francisco." Cape Mendocino was coined the "roughest and the highest station in California." The Trinidad Head lighthouse was the location of the largest wave ever recorded, and Punta Gorda was the "Alcatraz of Lighthouses." Each of these perspectives lends itself to an insight of the larger view of the first 100 years of Humboldt County lighthouse history. With the advancing industrial revolution and the onset of World War II, lighthouses along the Pacific Northwest were critical areas for protection and surveillance for attacks. By the 1950s, lighthouse keepers saw the end of an era, and most of the lighthouses became automated or closed.

In 1851, Navy lieutenant James Alden (pictured below), an assistant in the US Coastal Survey, sailed California's west coast in the ship *Active* looking for optimal lighthouse locations. Once he and his crew sailed through the Humboldt Bar, he reported that the best location for a Humboldt County lighthouse was on the north spit. He stated that "the north spit [is the] nearest point to the entrance, and is therefore, less liable to be obscured by fog." Ironically, on their return trip, his party was delayed 17 days because of fog and the roughness of the bar. Alden's decisions for a lighthouse location did not consider the shifting sands, isolation, weather, and geography. They would prove detrimental. (Both, courtesy of Library of Congress.)

Congress appropriated $158,000 in 1851 for seven lighthouses in California and three in Oregon. The Department of the Treasury awarded the contract to Gibson and Kelly, a contract firm from Maryland. Later, it was revealed that Gibson and Kelly bribed a treasury clerk $15,000 to be selected for the contract. However, the firm remained on the contract, and a provision was placed to eliminate any future conflicts of interest. Department of the Treasury architect Ami B. Young (pictured at right) designed the initial seven lighthouses, including the original one at Alcatraz (pictured above). The plans for all seven were identical with a Cape Cod design, living quarters on the first floor, and a lighthouse tower through the middle of the structure. (Above, courtesy of USLHS; right, courtesy of Library of Congress.)

The Humboldt Harbor Lighthouse was off to a rough start with delays in getting appropriations, building supplies, fraud, and retaining lighthouse keepers. From the outset, the ship *Oriole*, carrying building supplies for Cape Disappointment and Humboldt Harbor, wrecked as it was approaching the Columbia River bar in August 1853. All 20 workmen and the captain survived, however, that meant further delays for construction on both lighthouses. The Columbia River bar entrance was and is as dangerous as the Humboldt Bar. There were many more wrecks on the Columbia River entrance than Humboldt but that was due to higher traffic volume. Several ships, such as the 1930 *Admiral Benson*, have hit remains of other wrecks while entering the Columbia bar. (Above, courtesy of Friends of the Columbia River; below, courtesy of Keepers of the North Head Lighthouse.)

A few months after the *Oriole* disaster, another ship brought building supplies for the Cape Disappointment and Humboldt Harbor lighthouses. By 1853, most of the West Coast lighthouses that had been appropriated were complete. It would not be until 1854, though, that the Humboldt Harbor Lighthouse was finished and a few more years before it was lit. The location was remote, uneven, and over a mile from any supply ship. Planks were laid down in the soft sand to transport materials through the sand dunes. The lighthouse would cost the Department of the Treasury $15,000; it actually exceeded that price with an extension of the tower, thickening of the walls, and miscellaneous transportation costs for building a road to the site. However, a road was never built. (Courtesy of Palmquist Collection, Humboldt State University.)

During the completion of the California lighthouses, they transitioned from the US Lighthouse Establishment under the US Department of the Treasury to the US Lighthouse Board in 1852. Initially the lights were housed in parabolic reflectors (see example). However, with the transition to the US Lighthouse Board, all of the lights were required to have Fresnel lenses (see right) comprised of six orders, the first being the largest. The lens was named and designed by French physicist Augustin Jean Fresnel. The Humboldt Harbor light was furthered delayed from being lit when the lens that had to be imported from Sautter & Co. in Paris cost more than $3,000 and was instead shipped to Point Loma Lighthouse. It would be another year for the lens to reach the lighthouse in Humboldt Harbor. (Left, courtesy of Library of Congress; below, courtesy of Humboldt Maritime Museum.)

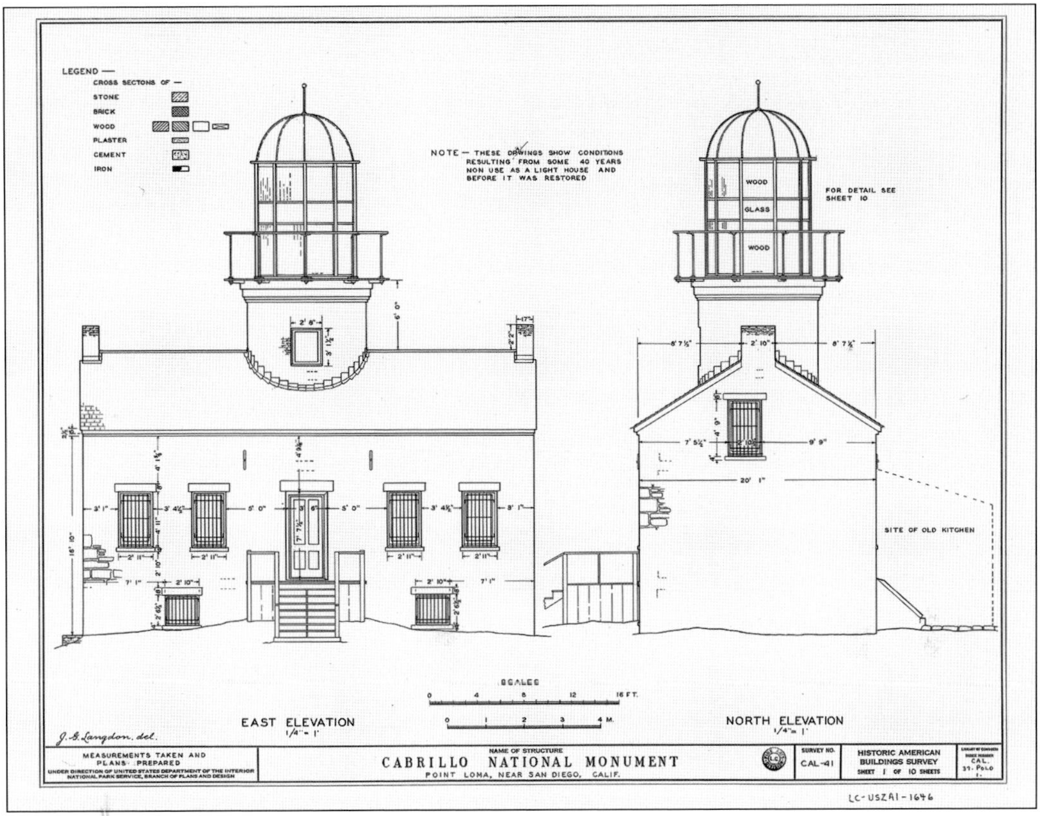

LEGEND — CROSS SECTIONS OF —
STONE
BRICK
WOOD
PLASTER
CEMENT
IRON

NOTE — THESE DRAWINGS SHOW CONDITIONS RESULTING FROM SOME 40 YEARS NON USE AS A LIGHT HOUSE AND BEFORE IT WAS RESTORED

WOOD
GLASS
WOOD
FOR DETAIL SEE SHEET 10

SITE OF OLD KITCHEN

SCALES

EAST ELEVATION 1/4" = 1'

NORTH ELEVATION 1/4" = 1'

J. G. Langdon, del.

MEASUREMENTS TAKEN AND PLANS PREPARED

NAME OF STRUCTURE
CABRILLO NATIONAL MONUMENT
POINT LOMA, NEAR SAN DIEGO, CALIF.

SURVEY NO. CAL-41

HISTORIC AMERICAN BUILDINGS SURVEY SHEET 1 OF 10 SHEETS

LC-USZA1-1646

Between Humboldt Harbor's first appropriation in 1851 and the official "Notice to Mariners" written by Maj. Hartman Bache published in the *Humboldt Times* on December 1, 1856, it had been a span of five years. The Humboldt citizens were in disbelief that the light was actually going to be lit. Bache writes, "The house is situated on the north sands, three-fourths of a mile from the inlet, and about midway between the bay and seashores. It consists of a keeper's dwelling of one story and a half, with a tower rising twenty-one feet above the roof from the center, both plastered and whitewashed and surmounted by an iron lantern painted red. The light is 53 feet above high water for spring tides and should be seen in clear weather from the deck of a seagoing vessel twelve nautical or fourteen stature miles." (Above, courtesy of USLHS; below, courtesy of HCHS.)

Selected in 1854, D.H. Pearce was first lighthouse keeper, but he grew impatient waiting for the light to arrive. Two years later, Capt. John Johnson was hired to replace him. Johnson; his wife, Sarah; and five children moved into the lighthouse quarters, which had two rooms on the bottom floor with a kitchen and an addition on the back. Johnson climbed the iron spiral staircase leading up through the tower on a cold winter night, December 20, to light the oil coal lamp. Nine months later, Sarah gave birth to their only daughter Sarah, named after her mother. (Sarah also had five other children from a previous relationship.) Shortly after the child's birth, Captain Johnson died of unknown causes. The lighthouse keeping became the responsibility of Sarah in addition to the care of her newborn and five other children. (Both, courtesy of USCG.)

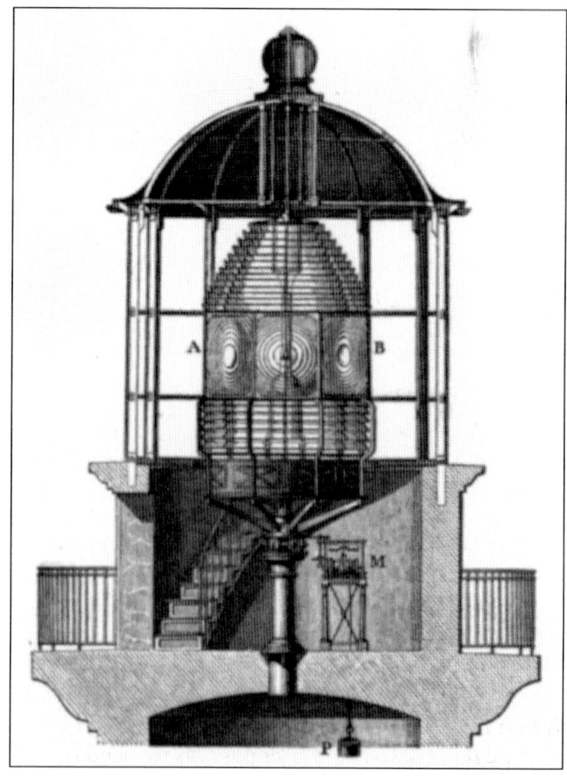

Ida Lewis, the lighthouse keeper of Lime Rock Island, Rhode Island, made her first drowning rescue in 1854 when she was 10 years old. When she was 14, she took over the lighthouse keeping from her father. Her lighthouse keeping tenure totaled 54 years of service, and she was credited with saving 18 people from drowning. She is famous as the first female recipient of the Gold Lifesaving Medal given to her by the US government in 1881 after she saved two soldiers who had fallen through ice. Lewis is also the most renowned woman lighthouse keeper of her time. Unfortunately, there were many women lighthouse keepers who went throughout history unnoticed and historically underpaid. After Sarah Johnson lost her husband, she took over as the lighthouse keeper at Humboldt Harbor from 1857 to 1863, all while raising her six children. When the US Lighthouse Board learned that Sarah had taken over her husband's official duties after he had passed away, her pay was reduced from $1,000 to $600 a month. (Courtesy of USCG.)

Old Fort Humbold, near Eureka, Cal. U. S. Grants headquarters 1853-1854.

During Sarah Johnson's tenure at the lighthouse, a dark period of Humboldt County history was literally unfolding in her backyard. The settlement of Humboldt Bay in 1850 and the displacement of indigenous people culminated in conflicts and unspeakable violence. In 1853, Fort Humboldt, built by the federal government to end these conflicts, never really helped. Instead, tensions escalated, and in February 1860, white settlers murdered 80–250 Wiyot women and children with axes, knives, and guns while they were at their world renewal ceremony. Unfortunately, there were very few survivors. One woman, Kaiquaish (also known as Josephine Beach), and her 11-month-old son William survived by not being on the island in the first place. Kaiquaish had set out in a canoe with her son to take part in the ceremony but became lost in the fog and was forced to return home before the attacks began. Josephine's son would later marry Maude Harrington, daughter of Trinidad Head Lighthouse keeper Fred Harrington. After the massacre, over 700 Indians were imprisoned and guarded on the north spit within a quarter mile of the lighthouse for almost three years. Sarah's tenure was within earshot of the massacres and proximity to the imprisonment. (Courtesy of Humboldt State University.)

After the death of Sarah Johnson's husband, she worked at the lighthouse for seven more years and became the longest keeper at the Humboldt Harbor Lighthouse. Not only was she keeping the light, but she also had to get all her supplies from across the bay in Eureka and take care of her young children. Supply runs entailed walking through sand, wading out to a moored rowboat, and rowing across the bay. In 1860, Sarah's oldest daughter Eliza married Joshua Van Sant, who was a prominent early pioneer and Eureka's town marshal. A year later, Sarah's first grandson Joshua Van Sant Jr. was born at the lighthouse and succeeded in becoming a professional photographer in Eureka. He photographed many Humboldt residents, including his own son William (pictured at right). Sarah retired in 1863 and died six years later of paralysis at the age of 43. She is buried in Myrtle Grove Cemetery and is commemorated each year. Of the keepers who followed her over the remaining 27 years, 19 resigned, 8 transferred, 7 were fired, 3 died, and 1 deserted. (Both, courtesy of the Palmquist Collection, Humboldt State University.)

The lighthouse was cursed from the beginning of its inception—ship captains had trouble seeing the light due to the tower's statue (53 feet above mean tide), one lighthouse keeper recorded 1,100 hours of fog in one year, there was constant flooding, and it was in a poor location. A wall of logs was constructed to act as a flood barrier for protecting the lighthouse foundation (pictured above). Earthquakes in 1877 and 1882 caused considerable damage to the lighthouse in which the south wall had been cracked, taken down, and rebuilt. In 1885, keeper William Price witnessed a cyclone hit the fog station and the lighthouse, ripping the roof off both structures. In 1885, it was decided that the combined tower and dwelling was unsafe for occupancy, and a new lighthouse was needed. (Both, courtesy of HCHS.)

In 1878, the Humboldt Life Saving Station was built to lessen the workload for the lighthouse keepers. The lifesaving station had a keeper in charge who trained and supervised surfmen responsible for rescues and assisting with the multitude of north coast shipwrecks. An 1883 drawing of the station was created by J.E. Mathews with the lifesaving station in the foreground, a shrubbed mound behind it, and the lighthouse in the background. The stations were equipped with self-bailing, self-righting lifeboats; surfboats; line-throwing Lyle guns; and surfmen. Today, the station has been rebuilt and has housed the US Coast Guard since 1939. (Above, courtesy of Palmquist Collection, Humboldt State University; below, courtesy of HCHS.)

With 1,100 hours of fog recorded in one year, Humboldt Harbor light was not as effective as the US Lighthouse Service wanted. There were 10 ships labeled "lost" between 1859 and 1873 when funding for a fog signal station was allocated. In 1872, a bell boat was staged in Humboldt Bay but lasted only two years. The original cost estimate for the fog signal building was $3,000, but the US Lighthouse Service received a bill for $6,000. Assistant lighthouse engineer E.G. Molera came up from San Francisco to investigate the discrepancy and found that the contractors were putting in tongue and groove flooring with layers of brick and cement mortar. The initial plans called for a dirt floor and no more than 16,000 board feet for the entire construction. Instead, the final product resulted in 58,000 board feet and a fog signal building that would withstand an eventual earthquake and cyclone. (Above, courtesy of USLHS; below, courtesy of Palmquist Collection, Humboldt State University.)

To mitigate the ineffectiveness of the lighthouse, a steam whistle was put in full operation on May 10, 1874. Running a steam-powered fog siren on the north spit turned out to be constant work. There were two keepers assigned to run the fog siren, and a shed was converted to a residence for one of the keepers and their family. The boilers required plenty of water and wood to keep it in operation. Three wells were dug, and the wood for the fire was transported across the bay. In 1883, an unusually foggy year required the 10-year-old boiler to be in constant use, and after 120 hours, the boiler failed. Ultimately, it was repaired, and the tugboats in the bay were saved from wrecking with one another. In 1889, the whistle hours were logged in at 1,189 hours, and the boiler consumed 111 cords of wood. A new fog station was built at the end of the north spit in 1906. (Both, courtesy of USLHS.)

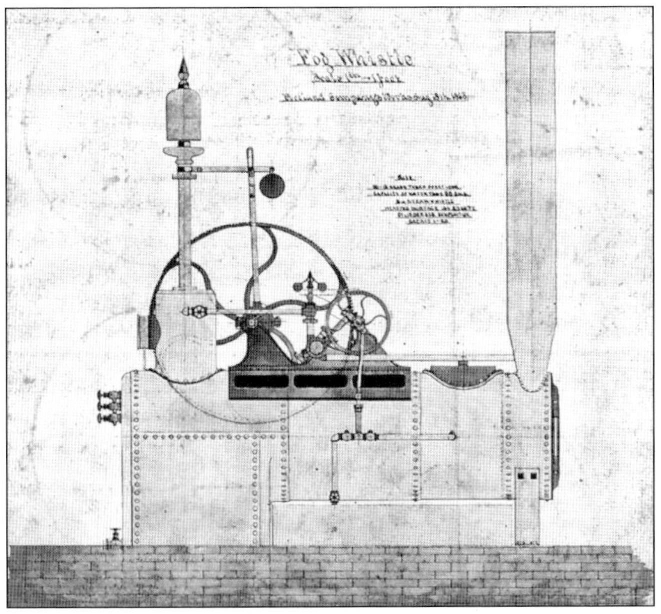

Humboldt Bay continued to be a busy harbor well into the 1930s. After the lighthouse was moved to Table Bluff, fog signal keepers were stationed at the north jetty. These men were called wickies and were responsible for keeping post lanterns filled with kerosene in order to burn five or six days. Every third day, they would boat out to each lantern and refill them and trim their wicks. The most difficult and dangerous light to maintain was on the south jetty. The spray from the jetty and the slippery surface was unstable for any seasoned wickie. Keepers also tended sound buoys that alerted mariners in foggy conditions such as Ballast Point (pictured at left). Bell boats, lightships, and harbor lights stretching from Eureka to Arcata were all instruments to assist vessels coming in and out of Humboldt Bay. (Both, courtesy of USLHS.)

In 1892, a new lighthouse was built at Table Bluff along with a keeper's dwelling and fog house. Originally, it was named Humboldt Bay Light Station, but the name was confused with the now defunct historical lighthouse. It was appropriately changed to Table Bluff Light Station, and in 1906, the Humboldt Harbor Lighthouse structure was ordered to be razed. However, it was left to crumble for many years, and in 1933, the entire structure collapsed. The original fourth-order Fresnel lens was moved to Table Bluff lighthouse, the oil lamp was moved to the San Francisco Bay Lighthouse Yacht Harbor, and the cupola can be seen today at the Humboldt Maritime Museum in Eureka. In 1920, *Humboldt Standard* journalist Frederick Schindler went into the decayed building, climbed the tower, and described what he saw: "Below us through the broken roof we see the flower-grown fireplaces, and a single joist still leading across from wall to wall as though to show that it was here the floor of this room used to be. Perhaps it was in that very room that J. Vansant, Jr., was born, some 50 years ago. A room that was then cozy and warm-and is now but a moss-grown fireplace and a single floor-joist, ready to crumble away at the least disturbance." (Courtesy of HCHS.)

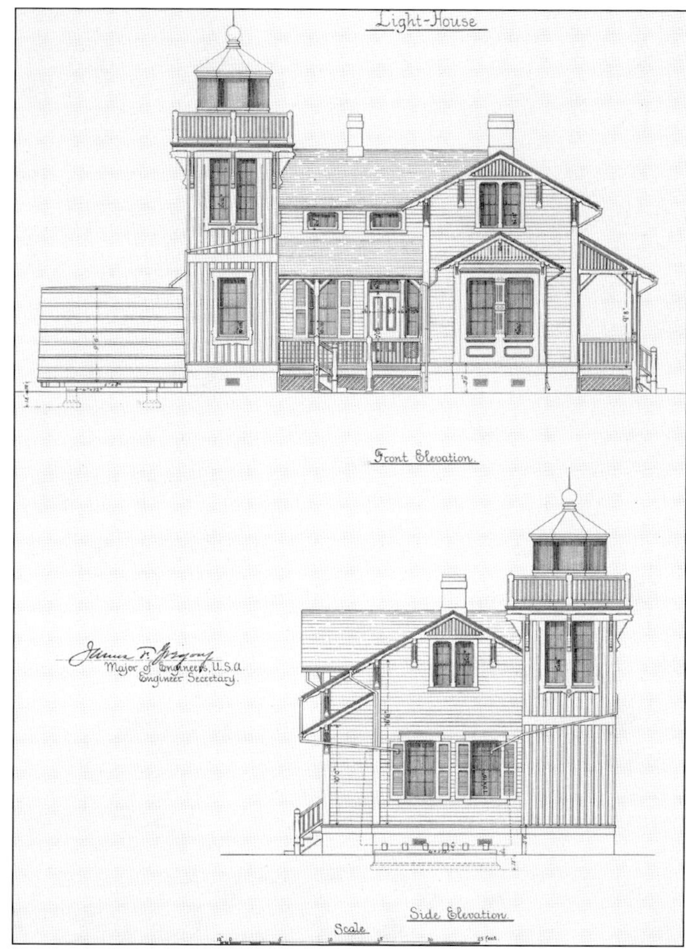

In 1892, the US Lighthouse Board made the decision to use Table Bluff for a new lighthouse location because it was midway between the Eel River and Humboldt Bay on an elevated bluff, making the light 200 feet above mean tide with a sweeping view of Eel River, which had considerable marine traffic. The light could be seen 20 miles in all directions. By the 1890s, the US Lighthouse Service knew what designs worked well for California lighthouses. Architects used San Diego's Ballast Point Lighthouse as the prototype for Table Bluff, while the keepers' house and the fog signal house were modeled after San Luis Obispo's design. After moving the fog signal station to the bluff, the board realized it was too far from the bay to be heard and relocated it back to the north jetty in 1906. (Left, courtesy of USLHS; below, courtesy of Palmquist Collection, Humboldt State University.)

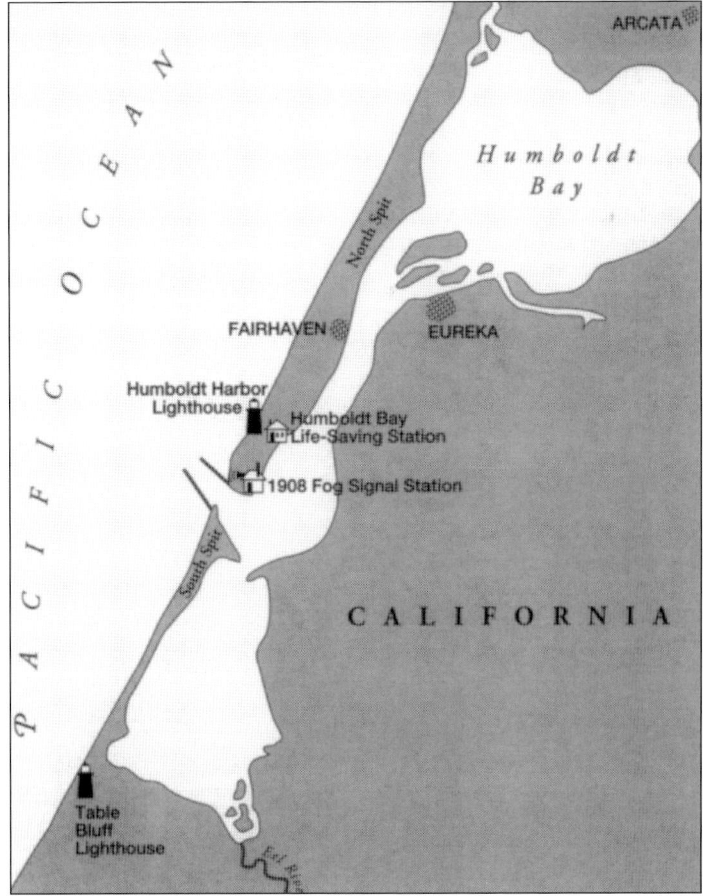

In 1890, Congress authorized funding for the Table Bluff Lighthouse Station at $25,000. The property owner wanted $5,000 for 10 acres, and the board thought this price was exorbitant and was prepared to exercise eminent domain when the owner reduced his price by half. By the early 1900s, the export of Humboldt County redwood dominated the West Coast market, especially after the 1906 San Francisco earthquake. After nearly 50 years of Humboldt Bay settlement, the bay was well fortified with a new fog signal station, a lifesaving station, and the Table Bluff Light Station. In 1909, a coast pilot described Humboldt Bay as "the first important harbor north of San Francisco," and the Humboldt Bay entrance "was dangerous to strangers." (Both, courtesy of USLHS.)

Table Bluff is 165 feet above the ocean. The light was 30 feet high, making the light 200 feet in elevation, a substantial improvement from the previous lighthouse. On the evening of October 31, 1892, head keeper Tony Schmoll lit the fixed, fourth-order Fresnel lens and mariners could see the light for 14 nautical miles. All the buildings were constructed to face the ocean, and the principal lighthouse keepers' house was attached to the tower, making it easy for them to keep the light going on stormy nights. There was also an assistant lighthouse keepers' duplex and a fog signal station to the left of the main house with a chimney that toppled in the 1920s due to an earthquake. There was a laundry house, an oil house, and a carpenter shop. This was not just a lighthouse but also a lighthouse station that encompassed several outbuildings and amenities for the keepers and their families. (Above, courtesy of USLHS; below, courtesy of Shuster Collection, Humboldt State University.)

The contract for all the outbuildings, lighthouse, and residences at Table Bluff totaled $18,000. The fog signal building was equipped with two steam generators that required a consistent supply of water from a spring nearby. A windmill was constructed to pump the water for an onsite tank. The station was extremely isolated from Eureka, but with 10 acres, there was plenty of room for the families to grow vegetables, raise chickens, and trade goods with the outlying community. After the advent of the automobile, Table Bluff and other lighthouses became a popular spot for visitors. According to a 1931 newspaper, "Visitors are welcome at Table Bluff and may inspect the lighthouse . . . on weekdays." However, weekends eventually became restricted because "there was such a rush that keepers were unable to attend to their required duties." (Above, courtesy of Lighthouse Friends; below, courtesy of University of California, Berkley.)

On December 20, 1941, the *Emidio* tanker was passing near Blunts Reef off Cape Mendocino when it was torpedoed by the Japanese. Coupled with the onset of World War II, this warranted significant response from the US Coast Guard. Table Bluff became an ideal place to operate a Navy radio compass station as well as house Coast Guard patrolmen and lookouts. A large barrack and six other structures were built for single men and married servicemen. Many of those assigned to the beach patrols traveled from the Midwest and had never been on a horse before. They took a seven-day train ride to California and went through six weeks of basic training in Alameda before heading north. They patrolled the beach on horseback from the bay entrance to the mouth of the Eel River, 12 hours a day. The nearby Table Bluff Hotel was also at full capacity with Coast Guard and Navy personnel. After the war in 1948, the Coast Guard razed some of the excess dwellings. The lighthouse keepers moved into the newer officers' quarters, and the original keepers' house that was attached to the lighthouse was also removed. (Courtesy of USCG.)

John Gonzales transferred to Table Bluff Lighthouse with his wife, Esther, in 1939 after serving at Fort Point and Piedras Blancas Light Station. He watched the Table Bluff swell with servicemen during World War II. During his last year on the bluff, 1948, his wife, Esther, answered a knock at the door. A commercial fisherman's boat, the *Pollyanna*, had gone ashore during the night on the south spit. The keepers—along with a Coast Guard crew, Coast Guard cutter, a bulldozer, and a jeep—were able to refloat the vessel. This was one of the last shipwreck events for the Table Bluff Light Station. John would eventually be promoted to principal lighthouse keeper in 1955 and transferred to Point Montara. By 1953, the fog signal was discontinued, and the lens was replaced by an automated 3.5-order Fresnel lens (pictured at right); it was eventually shipped to the Smithsonian in 1975. After the light was removed, new range lights were placed on both jetties, and an end of an era for lighthouse keepers on the north coast. (Above, courtesy of USLHS; right, courtesy of Smithsonian Institute.)

In 1969, pastor Ken Smith moved down from Oregon, purchased the 10-acre lighthouse station, and started a Christian community of young people (hippies). They lived on donated food and homegrown potatoes. Smith eventually grew tired of the cold bluff and moved to Hawaii in 1971. Local pastor Jim Durkin took over the mortgage payments and the preaching. Lighthouse Ranch was broadly known as a place to rehabilitate the youth from drugs, teach them to farm, and commit to Jesus. The Gospel Outreach community grew to well over 200 people, costing the organization $20 per person, per month. Durkin encouraged the collective to be creative, and they went on to forming the *Tri-City Advertiser*, which is now under the *Times Standard*. In 2005, Gospel Outreach sold 5.9 acres to the state, which in turn donated the land to the Bureau of Land Management. Waluplh/Lighthouse Ranch is surrounded by public preserves, an ecological preserve where a rare lily grows, Mike Thompson South Spit Wildlife Area, and the Humboldt Bay National Wildlife Refuge. (Courtesy of Jim Durkin.)

In 1987, the Table Bluff Lighthouse tower was cut in half and moved to the southwest end of Woodley Island Marina, where it can be seen today. The original Fresnel lens is now on display at the Humboldt Bay Maritime Museum near the Samoa Cookhouse. The museum also has the cupola from the original Humboldt Bay Lighthouse, which was found in the sand on the northern spit in 1987. In 2006, a replica of this tower was included in one of 28 Lake Havasu famous lighthouses reproductions and is located at the Lake Havasu Marina entrance. (Right, courtesy of Ray Glavich; below, courtesy of Lighthouse Friends.)

In 2012, all of the existing structures at Table Bluff were demolished, including the original water tower. The 57-foot structure was moved to the Bureau of Land Management's Piedras Blancas Light Station north of Cambria, California. The recycled redwood was used to replicate and restore the original 50-foot-tall water tower. The tower looks like an historic 20th-century water tower, and it also doubles as communications equipment that sends radio signals helping emergency crews communicate with one another, such as the California Highway Patrol, San Luis Obispo County Sheriff's Office, Caltrans, California State Parks, Cal Fire, California State Department of Fish and Wildlife, and the US Forest Service. (Left, courtesy of David Cooper; below, courtesy of BLM.)

The Bureau of Land Management awarded a contract for the demolition of all remaining structures on the property, including the original fog signal building, carpenter shop, oil house, and the foundation for the dwelling and tower. Unfortunately, the buildings were in a state of decay and well past the date for restoration. Visitors are now afforded an unobstructed view of the ocean while picnicking at the site. They can also enjoy a half mile walking tour with several interpretive trail signs describing the history of the lighthouse, Wiyot cultural history, natural and history as well as the marine protection area and the decades-long beach grass removal efforts on the south spit. (Both, courtesy of BLM.)

In 1602, the Spanish galleon captain Sebastian Vizcaino sent a letter to the viceroy of Spain letting him know that he was going to sail and explore the coast from Cape San Lucas to Cape Mendocino with two ships on an 11-month expedition. This was a frequented route during a time of Pacific Coast Spanish exploration. However, Cape Mendocino was usually avoided due to the geographic nature of the coast as the westernmost land point in the continental United States. The unpredictable currents, Blunts Reef, and the 326-foot sea stack "Sugar Loaf" were the cause of many shipwrecks during the mid-1800s and early 1900s. In 1860, the steamship *Northerner* hit a rock off the coast of Mendocino, claiming the lives of 38 people who washed ashore at Centerville Beach. (Above, courtesy of W.W. Elliott & Co.; below, courtesy of HCC.)

Lightships such as the *Swift Sure* served as mobile lighthouses up and down the coasts of the United States in the 1900s. They were often stationed in rocky areas such as Blunts Reef off the coast of Cape Mendocino. Although the Cape Mendocino lighthouse was in full operation, a lightship was stationed nearby beginning in 1905 until the 1950s. *Swift Sure* was present on the fateful day of June 15, 1916, when the steamer *Bear* carrying a crew and passengers ran aground at Bear River. The crew and passengers attempted to come ashore with lifeboats, but with the heavy surf, the boats capsized, and five people drowned. Those still aboard the *Bear* jumped in the remaining lifeboats and rowed out to the *Swift Sure* lightship for safety; 155 people sought temporary refuge. Without the assistance of the lightship, the passengers and crew would have most likely drowned, and it would have ended in one more tragic Humboldt County shipwreck disaster. (Courtesy of Kira Picabo.)

If there was ever a need for a lighthouse along the Pacific Coast, Cape Mendocino was at the top of the list. Rocky outcroppings, volatile seas, and gale winds caused a total of nine shipwrecks near its shores. However, getting the light and the structures built on the steep terrain proved to be even more difficult. In 1867, the lighthouse tender *Shubrick*, carrying the lighthouse and dwelling building supplies from San Francisco, went ashore 30 miles south of Cape Mendocino, near the area of Big Flat. All the materials were lost at sea, but the ship was saved and eventually repaired. New building supplies ultimately arrived, and the task at hand was getting the provisions up the steep switch backs. All materials were landed by sea and carried by pack mules, derricks, and humans up the steep hill where construction began. (Above, courtesy of USCG; left, courtesy of Ferndale Museum.)

Due to the steep terrain of Cape Mendocino, the building placement of the lighthouse, three keeper dwellings, and the barn and carpenter shop had to be bolted into the terraced hillside. Even then, the unstable ground made the original dwellings uninhabitable, and they eventually were razed. For many years, the assistant lighthouse keepers succumbed to living in the oil house. Breathing in the fumes of kerosene was dangerous and unhealthy for the keepers, and when the lighthouse inspectors came, they found that the keepers' health was either poor or in fair condition. Two new dwellings were built in 1908 that were like those at Punta Gorda and Point Cabrillo. These buildings were the highest lighthouse keepers' dwellings in the United States at 422 feet above the ocean. (Above, courtesy of Palmquist Collection, Humboldt State University; below, courtesy of USLHS.)

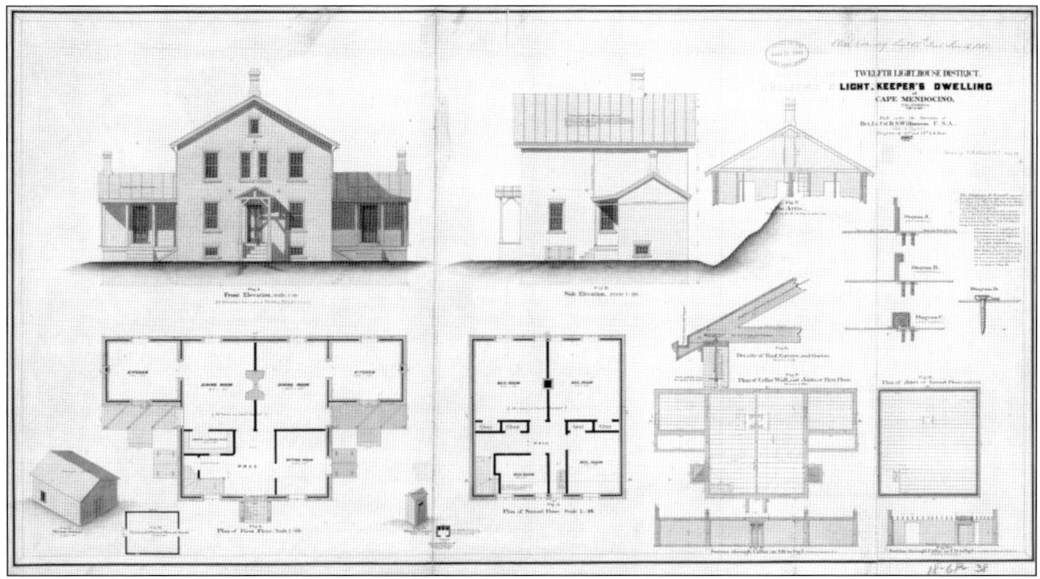

Cape Mendocino was known as one of the roughest stations to work and had one of the only first-order Fresnel lenses on the Pacific Coast. In 1867, the lens was shipped directly from a French company, L. Sautter, around Cape Horn to San Francisco and then carted by wagon to the lighthouse. The light was finally lit on December 1, 1868. Life at the station was extremely windy as described by the 1891 keeper, William Price: "Keeper vacating dwellings on account of the great portion of the roof blowing off, blowing the chimneys down . . . wrenching window shutters off their hinges." The keepers and their families sought refuge in the lighthouse and then moved into the barn on Christmas day. Depending on the day, many keepers had to run from their house to the lighthouse due to the high velocity of winds. (Left, courtesy of HCHS; below, courtesy of BLM.)

After the Japanese attack on Pearl Harbor on December 7, 1941, the Pacific Coast became a prime target and vulnerable to further attacks. Less than two weeks after the attack, the tanker *Emidio* was sailing from San Pedro to Seattle when it was struck by a Japanese torpedo 20 miles from Blunts Reef. Thirty-one survivors rowed 16 hours to the Blunts Reef lightship (pictured below) in Humboldt Bay. During this time, all Humboldt County lighthouses became monitoring stations for the military, and Cape Mendocino was no exception. After the war, the stations were continuously manned for another decade before the automation era began in 1950. (Above, courtesy of USCG; below, courtesy of Walter E. Frost.)

In 1948, the lighthouse was automated with a beacon, and the original lens was loaned to the city of Ferndale. For many years, Humboldt County fair attendees would reminisce about the 16 beams of light upon entering and exiting the weeklong summer fair event. In 2008, sixty years after the lens was moved from Cape Mendocino, the US Coast Guard assessed its condition and found that it was in "continued deterioration, due to a lack of a controlled environment, and the potential for further damage." The lens was removed from the replica lighthouse in September 2012 and placed in storage at the fairgrounds. (Above, courtesy of Ferndale Museum; below, courtesy of Barry Evans.)

In 1960, all of the structures—powerhouse, keepers' dwellings, oil house, and carpenter shed went up for auction with the contingency of moving the buildings. It had been a decade since the last keepers left the lighthouse, and the buildings were in poor condition with squatters living in them. Due to the lack of interest and buyers, the US Coast Guard burned all the buildings and in 1962 pushed the remnants off the cliff. The nonoperational lighthouse tower would stand alone for another 40 years. (Both, courtesy of MVHS.)

Forty years after the outbuildings were removed, the eroding landscape under Cape Mendocino lighthouse was slipping and taking the lighthouse with it. Without the intervention of multiple agencies, such as Humboldt County, the Bureau of Land Management, Army National Guard, Cape Mendocino Lighthouse Preservation Society (MLPS), and many volunteers, the lighthouse would be either rusted beyond repair or at the bottom of the Pacific Ocean. Volunteer work crews took apart the lower levels, unbolted 129 years of rusted pieces, and shipped them to Whitethorn Construction, where they were sand blasted and repainted. In 1998, the National Guard airlifted the lantern to Shelter Cove at Point Delgada in Mel Coombs Park. It was reassembled, painted, restored, and fitted with new glass by MLPS. Dedicated in 2000, it opened to the public on Memorial Day that same year. (Courtesy of BLM.)

In 1879, Charles Yale, secretary of the San Francisco Yacht Club, published a pamphlet titled *Pacific Coast Harbors*. In search of the ideal harbor between San Francisco and the Columbia River, he researched both the US Board of Engineer reports and sea captain oral interviews. He concluded that Trinidad was the ideal location for a harbor as it was 20 miles midpoint between the Columbia River and San Francisco. Although Humboldt Bay was the more frequented location, Yale and the board of engineers thought the cost of the jetties would be too much. They came up with a plan of enclosing the one-square-mile Trinidad Harbor with 1,000 tons of rock per day for 17 years at the cost of nearly $8 million. Yale's plan never gained traction, and in 1889, the effort and funds to build Humboldt Bay jetties was appropriated at $2.5 million. (Courtesy of Palmquist Collection, Humboldt State University.)

In response to the *Brother Jonathan* shipwreck near Crescent City in 1865, an appropriation for the Trinidad Head Lighthouse was made in June 1866 for 42 acres—the entire Trinidad Head. The construction of the concrete lighthouse, Colonial-style house, and cistern commenced in the spring of 1871 and was completed in the fall of that year. However, the fourth-order Fresnel lens was not officially lit until Jeremiah Kiler, principal lighthouse keeper, came to light it on December 1 of that year. He continued to service the light for 17 years until his death in 1888. (Left, courtesy of Swanlund-Baker Collection, Humboldt State University; below, courtesy of HCHS.)

Built on a 175-foot shelf, the Trinidad Head Lighthouse was the shortest tower on the north coast at 25 feet. It sat 200 feet above the ocean. Ships were able to see the fourth-order Fresnel lens up to 14 nautical miles. Each night before lighting the lantern, the wick was trimmed and cleaned. Every day at dawn, the curtains were drawn around the light because the glass would discolor in the sunlight. Initially, the station had one keeper, Jeremiah Kiler, and his wife, Sarah, as his assistant from 1800 to 1802. It would be another 26 years before a fog signal was put in place and assistant keepers would be added to the payroll. (Right, courtesy of HCC; below, courtesy of Trinidad Museum Society.)

The lighthouse site location was perfect for a light but lacked a year-round water source. From 1871 to the 1960s, water would be a constant issue. Initially, the US Lighthouse Service designed a catchment system off the lighthouse keeper's dwelling roof. Ten years later, a 6,000-gallon size tank was installed; by 1890, the area had a 10,000-gallon tank. During the summer months, with minimal rainfall, water was hauled by wagon a mile up from Trinidad or pumped from a ship offshore. In the 1930s, lighthouse keeper Malcolm Cady discovered a spring and pump, and concrete tanks were connected. Finally, in 1960, a water line was linked to the City of Trinidad. (Both, courtesy of the Trinidad Museum Society.)

To date, the Trinidad Head Lighthouse has the oldest California fog bell structure that is still standing and in operation. The station had no fog signal for its first 26 years and only one lighthouse keeper. In 1898, a 4,000-pound bronze fog bell arrived, and installation on the 126-foot cliff proved difficult. The bell was much like winding a clock, and it sounded every 10 seconds. In addition to keeping the light, the keeper had to run down the 48 wooden steps to the bell house and rewind the weights that hung down the cliff. Eventually, an assistant lighthouse keeper was hired for the additional workload. (Above, courtesy of HCHS; below, courtesy of USLHS.)

In 1900, shortly after the bell was installed, the wire weight cable snapped, and the apparatus plummeted 126 feet down to the ocean. Until it was repaired, the keeper had to ring the bells by hand. The US Lighthouse Service replaced the weights, but to avoid another catastrophe, they hired someone to build a tower to secure them (pictured at left). With the heavy winds and the sound of the bell producing strong vibrations, it caused the timers to fail. Warren Watkins (pictured below at right) was hired to anchor the tower into place. He secured himself by hanging by a rope over the cliff while he drilled holes into the rock. (Left, courtesy of HCC; below, courtesy of Boyle Collection, Humboldt State University.)

In 1899, Congress appropriated $250 to install a phone line connecting the keepers with the outside world. Sunset Telephone Company charged $60 a year in rental fees, and the board thought it was too costly and discontinued service in 1900. Shortly after, due to an increase in workload with the new fog signal, an additional keeper was hired and an added dwelling was allocated, built, and attached to the original structure in 1910. The keepers and their wives were important assets to the community of Trinidad, and they would often have visitors on Sundays after church and for special events. (Above, courtesy of Trinidad Museum Society; below, courtesy of Boyle Collection, Humboldt State University.)

Fred Harrington, lighthouse keeper from 1888 to 1916, was infamous for withstanding the largest wave in Humboldt County. In 1913, a 200-foot wave shook the lighthouse with such force, it put the light out. Harrington wrote about this event in his journal on that fateful date: "I was in the tower and had just set the lens in operation and turned to wipe the lantern windows when I observed a sea of unusual height then about 200 yards distant, approaching. I watched it as it came in when it struck the bluff; the jar was very heavy, and the sea shot up the face of the bluff and over it, until the solid sea seemed to me to be on a level with where I stood in the lantern (196 feet above mean high water). The whole point between the tower and the bluff was buried in water. The lens immediately stopped revolving and the tower was shivering from the impact for several seconds." (Above, courtesy of Palmquist Collection, Humboldt State University; left, courtesy of HCHS.)

By 1908, the Trinidad Head Lighthouse had been in operation for over 30 years. Here, Fred Harrington is standing overlooking the bluff as the Great White Fleet passed by the head in May of that year. Thousands of people came out to the Humboldt coast to witness 16 battle ships in the Great White Fleet voyage. This was a part of Teddy Roosevelt's campaign to send a message to Japan that America was prepared and equipped with a strong presence in the Pacific. The fleet began its route in Virginia, circled South America, and came north passing by the north coast to excited Humboldt County residents. This infamous photograph was taken by J.B. Meiser. (Above, courtesy of Thomas Hannah; below, courtesy of HCHS.)

In 1939, keepers throughout the United States made the transition from working as civilians for the US Lighthouse Service to either enlisting with the US Coast Guard or quitting. Many of them chose the latter, as World War II loomed in the distance. In 1947, the original Trinidad Head light was replaced by a 375-mm lens and an incandescent bulb, and the bell was replaced by an air diaphone. Both the bell and the light were donated to the Trinidad Civic Club. In 1949, the club designed and built a replica memorial lighthouse dedicated to those lost at sea. This lighthouse was officially named the Trinidad Memorial Lighthouse, but it was never operable. It was moved from its original location overlooking Trinidad Harbor to the base of Trinidad Head in 2018. (Both, courtesy of HCC.)

By the 1950s, almost all the lighthouses along the coast transitioned into automated lights. When the US Coast Guard became a permanent fixture on the head, the original keeper's dwelling was razed in 1961. In its place, the US Coast Guard built a triplex to house its personnel. The station became completely automated in 1974, but Coast Guard personnel continued to live in the housing until sometime after 2000. Between 2000 and 2002, the barracks were razed and the lighthouse remained, becoming the last operational lighthouse in Humboldt County. (Right, courtesy of Boyle Collection, Humboldt State University; below, courtesy of Tom Allan.)

After 145 years in operation, the US Coast Guard relinquished the 12 acres on Trinidad Head where the lighthouse resides to the BLM in 2014. The BLM, the City of Trinidad, the Trinidad Rancheria, and the Yurok tribe cooperatively developed the management plan allowing for public access to the site. The US Coast Guard continues to operate the navigational beacon with a fiber optic lens. The BLM partners with Trinidad Museum Society docents who lead lighthouse tours on the first Saturday of every month. The tours bring history to life and help connect families and children to the natural and cultural heritage of their public lands. For more information on special events and hours of operation, call the Trinidad Museum Society at (707) 677–3816. (Above, courtesy of Bob Wick; below, courtesy of BLM.)

With submerged rocks, fog, and the mountain shadows reflecting along the rocky coast between Shelter Cove and Cape Mendocino, the ocean had been a vortex for multiple shipwrecks. Between 1895 and 1907, ten ships met their end, including the *Chico* in 1906 and later the *Bear* in 1908 in Bear Harbor. Funding for lighthouses was much like traffic-light funding today; accidents and casualties prompted the need for safety measures, and funding ensued. In 1907, the steamer *Columbia* was heading north from San Francisco to Portland when it collided with the lumber ship *San Pedro*, and 77 people drowned. One year later, in 1908, tragedies like these motivated Congress to approve $60,000 for the construction of the Punta Gorda Lighthouse. (Above, courtesy of Swanlund Baker Collection, Humboldt State University; below, courtesy of HCC.)

Labeled the "Lost Coast," this area made the Punta Gorda Light Station the most remote lighthouse. It was coined the Alcatraz of the US Lighthouse Service, and the "foul balls" were stationed there as well as the "guys who had goofed off." Supplies arrived via a steam schooner off the coast of Fourmile Creek and were drug by horses a mile to the site. Several buildings were constructed on a level bench just above the high-water mark, including a fog signal structure, concrete oil house, blacksmith/carpenter shop, three two-story wood frame keepers' houses, and a barn. All but the fog signal and lighthouse were identical to Point Cabrillo Lighthouse. (Above, courtesy of USCG; below, courtesy of MVHS.)

On January 13, 1912, the fourth-order Fresnel lens was lit. Inside the lens was an incandescent oil vapor lamp. The oil lamp served as the light source for most of the 39 years during which the Punta Gorda Light Station was active. It could be seen 75 feet above mean high tide and for 14 nautical miles. An electric lamp came into use during the 1940s, only a few years before the light was permanently extinguished on February 15, 1951. (Above, courtesy of Russell Gilbert; right, courtesy of USLHS.)

Building the light station proved difficult but maintaining the structures and getting supplies proved long and arduous. Horses were invaluable transportation for the keepers whose preferred supply route came 11 miles from Petrolia. Wayne Piland, who had previously hung the harbor lights out at the Humboldt jetty, found that supplying Punta Gorda was "the toughest job you ever saw." The keepers had to get all of their winter supplies in by the first of November and all by horseback. Old Bill, the infamous horse from the San Luis Obispo lighthouse, transferred to Punta Gorda for 30 years and stayed longer than any resident. (Above, courtesy of MVHS; below, courtesy of USLHS.)

During the 1920s and 1930s, the lighthouse staff were not only hard workers but also creative. They were the only keepers in the country to use the fog signal station as an art gallery. Inside the signal station, visitors could see the fog signal compressor and all the impressive shiny brass tools such as lens cleaning materials, oil cans, and pitchers. This space was a visual experience amidst the backdrop of the keeper's landscape paintings that hung on the wall. Unfortunately, much of the art was solely seen by staff, and working at the lighthouse proved to be an isolating experience. Eventually, a phone line was put in with steel beams imbedded along Windy Point. (Both, courtesy of USLHS.)

In 1939, the Lighthouse Service management was transferred to the US Coast Guard and the keeper's life transitioned into a modern 20th-century world. The onset of World War II required frequent beach patrols, a newly constructed road, and electricity to Punta Gorda Lighthouse and dwellings. Before the road was built, keepers and their families such as Constance Lindley (pictured below) were only able to drive to Windy Point. In the 1940s, the US Coast Guard built a road from the mouth of the Mattole to Windy Point and then on to the lighthouse. The scout car (above) had large, oversized tires, which were deflated to navigate the beach sand. Coast Guard chief Samuel "Hank" Mostovoy (pictured above left) was the last head keeper of the Punta Gorda Lighthouse and said the generators did the "heavy lifting" but required 96 drums of fuel twice a year. (Both, courtesy of MVHS.)

Due to its remote location and high operating costs, in February 1951 Punta Gorda closed, and the light was removed and replaced by a lighted sound buoy just offshore. For 20 years, the vacant dwellings adjacent to the lighthouse remained with flowers blooming every spring and reminders of a time gone by. Groups of squatters took up residence in the 1960s and were determined to live in the vacant buildings. However, the buildings were in a constant state of decay and were dangerous. The BLM, fearing liability and with no plans for restoration, burned the wooden structures in 1970. Today, the cement light station and the oil house are all that remain and are located along the Lost Coast Trail in the King Range National Conservation Area. (Both, courtesy of MVHS.)

The BLM is dedicated to preserving the history and the structural integrity of both the lighthouse and the oil house. Both structures were nominated to the National Register of Historic Places under the significance themes of communications and transportation during the period from 1910 to 1951. In 2021, the BLM received Great American Outdoors Act funds to make repairs and stabilize both structures. Hikers are welcome to access this site and learn more about the history of Punta Gorda along the Lost Coast Trail in the King Range National Conservation Area. (Courtesy of BLM.)

Three

Lighthouse Life

Between 1856 and the 1950s, Humboldt County lighthouse keepers kept the light on at five different locations. They worked for the US Lighthouse Board under the Department of the Treasury and ultimately the US Coast Guard in 1939. Prior to lighthouse keeping, many served in the military during the Civil War, World War I, and World War II. The move from military life to lighthouse keeping was a natural fit, with round-the-clock workloads and frequent inspections. The keepers trimmed the wicks, fueled the light, cleaned the lenses and windows, kept the fog signal operable, and helped in rescue operations. In addition to keeping the light on, Humboldt lighthouse stations were equipped with fog signals, requiring a principal lighthouse keeper, a second assistant, and a third assistant. They made an average of $800 per year; lived in isolation; endured violent storms, earthquakes, and constant wind; and were self-sufficient and skilled at fixing equipment. Most of the keepers were men, but some were women who raised families in addition to performing their duties. It was typical to pass on the occupational "torch" of lighthouse keeping to succeeding members of the family. Many keepers' sons and daughters intermarried with other lighthouse keepers' families, and they generally transferred to other lighthouse stations in California. Depending on the location, their life and position were straightforward until the onset of World War II. Lighthouse stations along the Pacific Coast swelled with servicemen patrolling the beaches and conducting surveillance. Table Bluff Light Station saw new barracks constructed, and the keepers saw their post become an epicenter for servicemen with a much larger purpose. After the war, the lights were replaced with automatic lights, sound buoys, and jetty lights. By 1968, the Coast Guard initiated the Lighthouse Automation and Modernization Program (LAMP) to standardize all the remaining lighthouses to automation. Lighthouse dwellings were torn down, and keeping the light on became part of history.

Kaiquaish, also known as Josephine Beach (1839–1936), was born prior to the arrival of the Euro-Americans. At the time of her birth, there were 1,500 Wiyot people. When she was 21 years old, on February 25, 1860, she and her 11-month-old son were canoeing to Tuluwat (Indian Island) for the Wiyot world renewal ceremony that would last 10 days. This was a yearly event that included dressing in traditional Wiyot regalia as well as singing and dancing. Fortunately, she became lost

in the fog and returned home. On February 26, 1860, at 6:00 a.m., Euro-Americans arrived on the island and murdered 80 to 250 women, children, and older men. This event, called the Indian Island Massacre, was one of many attacks that week. After the 1860 Indian Island Massacre, few tribal members remained. Kaiquaish and her 11-month-old son were two of the few women and children who survived this horrific event. (Courtesy of Jenni Kupelian.)

Josephine Beach's father was Kiwelta, the Wiyot chief who met with the Josiah Gregg party when they "discovered" Humboldt Bay in 1850. Kiwelta's portrait was painted by Stephen W. Shaw, a forty-niner portrait painter who was instrumental in helping name Humboldt Bay and one of the first pioneers who entered the bay on the *Laura Virginia* in 1850. Shaw painted this portrait in 1852, and it hangs in the Clarke Museum today. His daughter Kaiquaish, also known as Josephine Beach, married Charles Beach at the age of 17 and had 12 children. Josephine and Charles's son Robert Beach married Maude Harrington, daughter of Trinidad Head Lighthouse keeper Fred Harrington. During this period of time, the community of Humboldt County was relatively small, therefore, connections between lighthouse keepers as well as the blending of cultures was a relatively common occurrence throughout Humboldt County. (Courtesy of Society of Humboldt Pioneers.)

Fred Harrington's life encompassed a rich period of American history, the industrial revolution, Civil War, and westward expansion. Harrington's father, Benjamin, capitalized on the 1849 Gold Rush period as job opportunity and moved his family from Boston, Massachusetts, to San Francisco in 1852. Overnight, San Francisco went from a population of 1,000 in 1848 to 25,000 in 1849. Benjamin did not go into the goldfields but used his stone-cutting skills to help build the booming city. Fred was nine years old when they moved from Massachusetts, and he was enrolled into one of the seven grammar schools in San Francisco, the oldest being Spring Valley Science School, which is still in existence. In 1860, when Fred was 17, he got his first job as a clerk. This was on the eve of the Civil War, and it predominated the American landscape. (Courtesy of the Trinidad Museum Society.)

Fred Harrington enlisted in Company C, 2nd California Infantry Regiment on December 29, 1864, assembled in the Presidio, San Francisco. The company was ordered to the Arizona Territory in 1865 to provide security for a steadily increasing stream of settlers and miners into the area, both before and after the Civil War. Like Humboldt County during this period, the newly developed states such as Arizona were battle zones between the native tribes and the settlers and prospectors. Harrington was eventually promoted to full command sergeant in April 1866 and mustered out in May of that year. In 1875, at the age of 34, he married 17-year-old Josephine Evans and two years later had a son, Frederick Arthur Harrington. Ultimately, Fred's dream job was to be a principal lighthouse keeper. (Courtesy of the Trinidad Museum Society.)

After Fred Harrington left the military in 1865, he worked as a clerk for John Stratman, a wholesale news dealer in San Francisco, a bookkeeper, a laundryman in Eureka, and as a San Quentin prison guard for two years starting in 1880 in which the family lived in San Rafael (pictured above). As an experienced prison guard and Army sergeant, his credentials as a second assistant lighthouse keeper at Cape Mendocino in 1882 was a natural fit. Before Harrington came to Cape Mendocino, they had eliminated the third assistant position when the fog signal was discontinued in 1873. Many lighthouses had four keeper positions depending on the workload, and the principal lighthouse keeper could hire or fire his assistants at will. Ultimately, the decision to hire Harrington was subjected to approval from the US Lighthouse Board inspector based in San Francisco. From 1868 to 1910, operations were administered by the US Lighthouse Board under the Department of the Treasury. (Courtesy of Marin Free Library.)

In 1888, Fred Harrington was promoted to principal lighthouse keeper at the Trinidad Head Lighthouse after six years as second assistant at Cape Mendocino (1882–1885) and first assistant at Piedras Blancas (1886–1888). During the winter months, if the "light up" time was 6:00 p.m., the second assistant who was on duty from noon to 6:00 p.m. would prep the lighthouse with lanterns at 4:00 p.m. to ensure that the light had plenty of kerosene, the lighthouse was clean, and the wicks were trimmed. Harrington would light the lamp and take the watch from 6:00 p.m. to midnight until his assistant took over from midnight until 6:00 a.m. Once the light was out, everything had to be cleaned, polished, and ready to go for the evening. Harrington earned $800 per year but ultimately got $1,000 with 18 years of tenure until his death in 1916. (Courtesy of Boyle Collection, Humboldt State University.)

UNITED STATES
LIGHT HOUSE SERVICE.

SECOND DEPUTY
JAN 4 1899
COMMISSIONER

Trinidad Head
Light House Station,
HUMBOLDT COUNTY, CAL.

Trinidad, Dec 17- 1898

Hon John H Barham
Washington D.C

Dear Sir:

In reference to the rejected claim for increase of pension of Mr James T. Lee a Mexican Veteran whom You met while in Trinidad in last Oct. I would like to submit the following facts which it was not concidered necessary to show in his application. and which would very probably make a deference in the decision of the Commissioner -

The land on which he lives while, standing in his name on County records is actualy owned by the following parties Geo Brooks 25 acres - Tilford Lee 40 acres - and the ballance in equal proportions by Belle - Thomas and Mrs Lee (wife of applicatant. the land does not furnish any of them a living and only stands in applicants name to save the expense of surveying and deeding - all taxes are paid by them. All personal property now owned by applicant is 6 sheep -

As a resident of Trinidad, Fred Harrington was a vital community member and was in a position of authority. In 1898, he wrote a letter on US Lighthouse Service stationary (above) to the pension commissioner, John Barham, in support of a Patrick's Point resident, James Tilford Lee (1821–1903), an "old soldier." Lee was a Mexican war veteran who was seeking a pension raise from $8 to $12 per month. The land on which Lee was living was considered part of his income; however, it was owned by other people, and Harrington was correcting those assumptions in his letter. Harrington kept a daily log as a part of his lighthouse keeping duties in which he recorded the weather, ocean tides, and his daily duties. He was known and regarded by his superiors to be immaculate in his writing skills and his position as a lighthouse keeper as well as conscientious. (Courtesy of Lee Ann Shnayer Collection.)

Josephine Evans (1858–1937), born in Des Moines, Iowa, came to California with her parents as a young woman in 1870. Her father, George Evans, was a ferryman in San Francisco, and they lived off Market Street. In 1875, at the age of 17, she married Frederick Harrington and had three children, Maude, Frederick Jr., and Clinton. Her life changed dramatically once she moved from San Rafael to Cape Mendocino in 1882 with two toddlers ages two and five. The only community was the keepers and their families. By the time they came to Trinidad (population 100) in 1888, it was a breath of fresh air. The constant wind of Mendocino had subsided, and her community had expanded. Josephine's sole responsibility of taking care of her children and the house increased remarkably once she took on lighthouse keeping responsibilities. Also part of her duties was to host any visitor who came up the wagon road for a day at the lighthouse. She was known by many Trinidad residents to be a hard worker who succeeded her husband by many years. She passed away at the age of 79 and is buried at the Trinidad Cemetery. (Courtesy of Jenni Kupelian.)

When the Harrington family moved onto Trinidad Head in 1888, they were the second lighthouse keepers, succeeding Jeremiah Kiler. They moved into the single-family dwelling, built in a Colonial-style architecture and perched on the cliff overlooking the ocean. They lived at the Trinidad Light Station for 28 years, the longest lighthouse keepers on the head. Compared to the other lighthouses, Trinidad, however isolating, was in fairly sheltered area compared to the Punta Gorda and Mendocino Light Stations. The family lived there until Fred passed away in 1916. Although Josephine did not hold the official title of lighthouse keeper, she helped Fred with his duties in trimming and cleaning the lamp wicks, cleaning the windows, sounding the bell, updating the logs, fetching water, and raising their children. (Courtesy of Keystone Collection, University of California, Riverside.)

In 1890, Maude Harrington was 10 years old and attending the one-room schoolhouse with her brothers Fred and Clinton. Due to the limited population of Trinidad, the entire student body attended a one-room schoolhouse. In addition to schoolwork, Maude was responsible for helping her mother with household duties such as sewing, washing, and dusting. In 1897, when she was 17, she left the small town of Trinidad and went to Fresno Business School with a population of 12,000. The business school was where bookkeepers and "typewriters," as secretaries were called then, were trained. She was gone for a few years and then returned to the comfort and familiarity of Trinidad, her family, and the friends she grew up with. (Courtesy of MVHS.)

By 1902, Maude Harrington was back at the Trinidad Head Lighthouse, where she would meet the man she would marry, Perry Hunter. Eventually, he became the father of her two boys, Milton and Ralph. Perry, the son of Paschal Hunter, Table Bluff Lighthouse keeper, heard that Fred Harrington needed an assistant keeper. Perry was reported to have ridden up on his horse with a fiddle on his back. He was such a good fiddle player that he wooed both Fred and Maude and got the job. Fred not only hired him but also called up the planner for the Temperance Hall and offered Perry's services for the upcoming dance. A year later, Perry and Maude eloped in San Francisco and moved to Point Reyes Lighthouse for two years and then Cape Mendocino, where they had their two boys, Milton and Ralph. Maude grew tired of the isolation and went back to Trinidad Head with her parents. Maude and her parents raised her boys at the lighthouse until 1916, when her father died. Milton and Ralph witnessed the 200-foot wave hitting the lighthouse in 1914 with their grandfather at the helm. Years later, Maude married Robert Beach, the grandson of Wiyot chief Kiwelta. An autograph book dated 1894 was recently uncovered in which Maude copied the fitting poem called "Live for Something" by Robert Whitaker to her friend Mary. (Courtesy of Mary Spinas Kline Collection, Trinidad Museum.)

Perry Hunter was born and raised in the Mattole Valley in the late 1800s. His father, Paschal Hunter, was originally a rancher and then became second assistant lighthouse keeper at Table Bluff Lighthouse in 1897 when Perry was 15. Perry lived with his father, mother Alice, and sister Edna at the Table Bluff Lighthouse until he was old enough to be a lighthouse keeper himself. In 1902, at the age of 19, he was hired by Fred Harrington, keeper at the Trinidad Head Lighthouse. Fred's assistant had quit, and Fred had put the word out to the other keepers that he needed help. Perry, jobless but with lots of experience, was no stranger to lighthouse keeping and was hired as a laborer for one year before he married Fred's daughter Maude. They eloped in San Francisco, and Perry transferred to Point Reyes Lighthouse and then on to Cape Mendocino Lighthouse with Maude and his new family. (Courtesy of MVHS.)

Perry Hunter was a bit of a Peter Pan; he held nine appointments during his lighthouse career along the Pacific Northwest. When he left Trinidad, he went to Cape Mendocino and then transferred to Pigeon Point, Point Reyes, Punta Gorda (pictured here with his aunt), and then made a full circle back to Trinidad Head, retiring in 1946 as principal lighthouse keeper for the US Coast Guard. Hunter had enlisted in the Coast Guard in 1939 when President Roosevelt consolidated the US Lighthouse Service. In between lighthouse keeper positions, he left the US Lighthouse Service in 1909 and joined a crew on the steamship *Roanoke*, which hauled passengers and cargo up and down the Pacific Northwest coast, until it ultimately sank in 1916. Hunter also worked on Alcatraz as a laundry supervisor for the prison. He and Maude Harrington Hunter were only married a short time, but he eventually remarried at the age of 58. Hunter died in 1959 at 76 years old and is buried in the Golden Gate National Cemetery. (Courtesy of MVHS.)

Paschal Hunter and his family were one of the first pioneering ranching families in the Mattole Valley. Paschal's father, Walker Hunter, was a rancher who left Missouri in 1855 with his new bride, Nancy, and settled near the town of Petrolia. In 1909, Walker applied for and received public domain land administered by the General Land Office. The parcels were available for homesteaders who could make a sustainable living off the land that they managed. Ultimately, the acreage that was not claimed became public land under the General Land Office and is now managed by the Bureau of Land Management. Paschal continued the family tradition of ranching until he set his sights on other opportunities, such as a civil servant lighthouse keeper. He got his opportunity to be the second assistant lighthouse keeper at Table Bluff in 1897 for $550 a year. (Courtesy of the MVHS.)

Lighthouse keepers were transferred or promoted to different locations often. Paschal Hunter was offered a promotion from second assistant lighthouse keeper at Table Bluff Lighthouse to first assistant lighthouse keeper at Cape Mendocino in 1903. He was at Table Bluff for nine years and laterally transferred in 1912 to the newly built Punta Gorda Lighthouse, his home base. He and Fred Arthur Harrington (pictured), son of Fred Harrington, Trinidad lighthouse keeper, lit the light inside the fourth-order Fresnel lens together for the first time on January 15, 1912. Unfortunately, Hunter died of a heart attack three months later in April at the age of 55 and is buried at the Petrolia Pioneer Cemetery. (Courtesy of MVHS.)

Fred Arthur Harrington, son of Fred Harrington, keeper of the Trinidad Lighthouse, moved from Cape Mendocino to Trinidad Head Lighthouse with his parents and siblings when he was 11 years old. He and his two siblings, Maude and Clinton, shared in lighthouse keeping duties while living in the beautiful Colonial-style house. As a young man, Fred served as an unofficial assistant lighthouse keeper with his father at the Trinidad Head Lighthouse. In 1900, he and his wife, Edna Hunter, pictured here newly married, moved to Fort Point, where he became an official first assistant lighthouse keeper. Edna was the daughter of Punta Gorda Lighthouse keeper Paschal Hunter. Fred and Edna had two children together, and he spent his entire working career at various lighthouse locations along the Pacific Northwest. (Courtesy of MVHS.)

Fred and Edna Harrington had two children, Donald and Jesse. When Jesse was born in 1901, Fred and his family transferred to Alcatraz Lighthouse Station (pictured) as first assistant lighthouse keeper. He then transferred to Point Reyes in 1903 for two years as a second assistant and accepted a promotion at Table Bluff Lighthouse in 1905 when his son Donald was five. In 1911, he was transferred as principal lighthouse keeper to the new Punta Gorda Light Station with his father-in-law, Paschal Hunter. He was at Punta Gorda for eight years and returned to Alcatraz Lighthouse Station in 1919 as principal keeper for 19 years until his death at the age of 61 in 1938. In 1963, after the penitentiary closed, the lighthouse became automated, and a modern beacon was added. (Courtesy of California State University Library.)

Sarah Johnson, a native of Belfast, Ireland, left her home for the coast of Australia with her first husband, William John McKenna. McKenna was a carpenter by trade and built houses for the ever-growing population of Australia. By 1849, Sarah and William were ship bound for California with three children and one on the way. William got a job in Benicia as a carpenter, but it was short lived. The family moved to Eureka after William was offered a job to help build Fort Humboldt. Sarah divorced William during this time and was living in Eureka with her five children on her own. In 1856, she married W. John Johnson, who became the first keeper at the Humboldt Harbor Lighthouse. Unfortunately, Captain Johnson died the following year in 1857. Two weeks before he died, he was able to see his newborn daughter Sarah Elizabeth (pictured). (Courtesy of Melvin Shuster.)

With her husband's passing, Sarah Johnson became the principal lighthouse keeper at Humboldt Harbor Lighthouse for six years while also taking care of her six children. Her oldest boys—Alex, 12, and James, 11—presumably assisted with her lighthouse-keeping duties. In addition to her paid duties, Sarah had to settle John's estate, and shortly after he passed, she invested in property near Bucksport. When the US Lighthouse Board found out officially that her husband had died, they reduced her pay by almost half. She was the longest tenured principal lighthouse keeper, and just before she retired in 1863, she witnessed two major shipwrecks coming in and out of the Humboldt Bar, the *Aeolus* and the *Merrimac*, where everyone on board was lost at sea. She died of paralysis in 1869 and was buried at Myrtle Grove Cemetery in Eureka. The US Coast Guard honors Sarah Johnson every Memorial Day by placing a lantern and an American flag on her grave. (Courtesy of Peg Wheeler.)

George Cobb is pictured at 23 years old when he started his career as an assistant lighthouse keeper at Oakland Harbor. Cobb came to work at the new Humboldt fog station in 1908 as principal lighthouse keeper. The station was located at the cypress grove picnic area at the Samoa Dunes Recreation Area. The trees were planted for shrubbery to delineate the boundaries between the two keepers' houses. Cobb worked at the fog station for nine years, which was longer than most. Due to the remote location of the north spit, the constant fog, and the exhausting commute for supplies in Eureka, the turnover rate was high. There were no roads around the bay, and the only ferry service was from Samoa, four or five miles away. Each keeper had their own rowboat and rowed across the bay to Bucksport for shopping and errands. Cobb was transferred to Fort Point in 1917. His last post was in San Diego at Point Loma (an identical design to Humboldt Harbor). By the time his career ended, he had served 43 years with the US Lighthouse Service and the Coast Guard along the Pacific Coast. He had served longer than any other lighthouse keeper at the time of his death. During his tenure, he saved eight lives from drowning and was awarded a medal from Congress for distinguished service. (Courtesy of USLHS.)

Stephen Pozanac, a Czech immigrant, came to the United States in 1890 and eventually served in the US Army during World War I. He was stationed at Fort Barry, near Point Bonita Light Station. He became so familiarized with the lighthouse keeper's way of life that he made it his career goal after he left the service. He met his wife, Minnie, the daughter of a Lime Point lighthouse keeper, and in 1919, he and Minnie moved to Ano Nuevo Island, where he took the second assistant lighthouse keeper position. On the remote Ano Nuevo Island, near San Francisco Bay, Minnie gave birth to their only son Thomas in an elaborate seven-room lighthouse keeper dwelling. The Coast Guard closed the light station in 1948 and sold it to the State of California in 1955. It is now a wildlife preserve providing habitat for sea birds and elephant seals. Stephen is standing next to a fifth-order Fresnel lens manufactured in Paris, France, which was first exhibited on August 5, 1890. (Courtesy of USLHS.)

In 1922, Stephen Pozanac was promoted to first assistant lighthouse keeper and moved to Table Bluff Lighthouse with a salary of $840 per year. He and his wife, Minnie, supplemented their income with a large garden of vegetables and chickens, and they had enough left over to sell to markets in Eureka. One night in 1923, Stephen was making his way to his post to stand watch when a strong earthquake struck the station, toppling the chimney on the fog signal building and sending it crashing through the roof. The pile of bricks landed right where Stephen would have likely been standing watch. He and his family moved to Ballast Point Lighthouse in San Diego in 1938, where he was promoted principal lighthouse keeper. He retired from service in 1945 and lived to be 103 years old. He died on Christmas day in 1988. (Courtesy of University of California, Berkeley.)

Charles Lindley was born in Connecticut and came out to San Diego, California, with his British-born parents in 1881. His father was a farmer by trade, and Lindley eventually became a blacksmith for 10 years under the US Engineer Corps. Working for the government and in engineering, he saw that the combination was well suited to becoming a lighthouse keeper. In 1907, he began work at the New Point Loma Lighthouse in San Diego, and by the age of 46 in 1920, he was working as a first assistant lighthouse keeper at East Brother Island in San Rafael. In 1921, Lindley and his wife, Constance, moved to the remote Punta Gorda Lighthouse, where he accepted the position of second assistant lighthouse keeper for three years and was eventually promoted to principal lighthouse keeper. (Courtesy of MVHS.)

Charles and Constance Lindley were at the Punta Gorda Lighthouse during the powerful 1923 7.2 magnitude earthquake that cracked the foundation of the principal keepers' house. It triggered some environmental hazards such as mercury spilling in the lighthouse and about 30 gallons of oil sloshing out of the oil tanks in the oil house. During Charles's tenure at the lighthouse, all supplies were brought in by horseback, 11 miles one way. Three years before his retirement in 1935, the government built a road to Windy Point, shortening travel time and travel methods (automobile) from Petrolia to the lighthouse. He and his wife were at the Punta Gorda Lighthouse Station for nearly 20 years until 1938 when Charles retired. Charles died of a stroke in 1957 in San Francisco, and his wife, Constance, died one month later. They had no children and are both buried at Ocean West Cemetery in Eureka. (Courtesy of MVHS.)

Coast Guardsman Ronny Thomas is shown at left driving the scout car at Punta Gorda Lighthouse in 1949; the others are unidentified. Thomas was a 17-year-old from Los Angeles who wore platform shoes to meet the Coast Guard's height requirement and was assigned to Punta Gorda Lighthouse in November 1949. He embarked on a steamship from San Pedro and sailed up the coast to Humboldt Bay. Coast Guardsman Paul Blossfield picked Thomas up and drove him to the Mattole River, where they met the lighthouse station's three horses: Tom, Jerry, and Bill. Thomas's sea bag was loaded into the pack saddles, and the horses were set free. Thomas asked Blossfield how far it was to the lighthouse. "Seven miles," responded Blossfield. Thomas later recounted that he thought his sea bag was lost forever. Many of the young men who enlisted in the US Coast Guard after the war had never been around horses much less the remote area of the Lost Coast. (Courtesy of MVHS.)

When Ronny Thomas arrived at the lighthouse station and was shown his living quarters, he was pleasantly surprised to see all of his clothes hung up and his items put away. He wondered for years how the horses opened and closed all the gates leading to the lighthouse. Jack Evenden was responsible for hauling supplies with the station's horses (pictured) from Petrolia south to the station. In the winter months, a keeper would have to wait in between storms to ride into Petrolia for mail and provisions and head back before the weather turned for the worse. The most famous horse was Old Bill, who arrived on a lighthouse tender and served for more than 30 years, longer than any human resident. Apparently, Old Bill was afraid of water and would try to jump even the smallest puddle. When he was hitched to a wagon, it was even more dangerous, and many keepers would just walk than deal with Old Bill. (Courtesy of MVHS.)

Jackson Fletcher Wills spent his military career in the Spanish-American War in 1892, was promoted to sergeant, and mustered out 12 years later in 1904 in San Francisco. He was born and raised in West Virginia, but once he was in California, he stayed for the duration of his life. Like other contemporary lighthouse keepers, his background was military, and it was a perfect fit. He got married just after the 1906 earthquake and worked at Mare Island in Vallejo until he started his career as a third assistant lighthouse keeper at Point Sur in 1913. The light was a first-order Fresnel lens that had a 450-pound weight suspended beneath the lens. After being cranked up by the keeper, it would rotate the lens for four hours. Wills's job was most likely keeping the steam-powered whistle fed with fuel as it had five-second blast every 35 seconds. Life at the lighthouse was extremely isolating, as there was no Highway 1 until the 1930s. (Courtesy of USCG.)

Fletcher Wills transferred to the remote Punta Gorda Light Station as second assistant lighthouse keeper in 1913 and was there for two years before transferring to Table Bluff in 1915. He was eventually promoted to first assistant and ended his keeping career in 1920. During these position changes, his children went to boarding school in Petrolia and later Fortuna and Table Bluff. Wills's goal was to be a permanent civil service employee, and he eventually became a prison guard at San Quentin. The family lived in housing there for six years, and it was there that Wills took up the art of making violins. He ended his working career as a watchman at Pier 17 in San Francisco. He and his wife are buried at the Golden Gate National Cemetery in San Francisco. (Courtesy of MVHS.)

Capt. Archibald Philander Marble (b. 1831), a native of New York, arrived in California in 1852. He mustered into Company K, 2nd California Infantry Regiment on December 5, 1861, serving at Fort Humboldt for four years and later coming back to be Humboldt Harbor's principal lighthouse keeper from 1869 to 1874. During his last year, his wife, Mary, worked as his assistant. In 1872, Archibald was accused of "drunken disregard of his duties," and he was "incapacitated from properly discharging the duties of such Light Keeper." He was sued for libel when there was an absence of light on several occasions. Two years later in 1874, he and his wife moved to the remote Cape Mendocino. Mary was there for only one year, and the couple later divorced. In addition to the lighthouse, there was a signal station and keepers' dwellings. Archibald was married four times (once for only a few days), and he had eight children. (Courtesy of HCC.)

Cape Mendocino Lighthouse was built to mitigate the many shipwrecks that occurred in the vicinity of the Cape. Unfortunately, it was not enough to stop the continuous wrecks, including the steamship *Bear*, seen above, in 1918. Ironically in 1881, while Archibald Marble was the lighthouse keeper, one of the ships that wrecked was carrying the lighthouse inspector, who drowned upon arrival. Marble was labeled and known to be a scurrilous lighthouse keeper of the Pacific Northwest's wild coast. However, to his credit, he was by far the longest tenured lighthouse keeper at the Cape, serving nearly 15 years. Most lighthouse keepers only endured two years at the Cape. The post was the most arduous, strenuous, isolating in all of Humboldt, and his short-lived marriages reflected it, one of them lasting just nine days. The *Humboldt Times* reported the ill-fated marriage: "Miss Louise Harding stepped off the Humboldt vessel, it was announced that the lady would soon become Mrs. Marble. The happy couple left shortly afterwards for their home at Capetown. The blissful honeymoon was unfortunately destined to exist only nine days, & the blooming young bride has gathered up her grips & tried herself back to the busy thoroughfares of the Golden Gate city." (Courtesy of HCC.)

Life at Trinidad Head Lighthouse was fairly isolated; however, it was the most coveted post in all of Humboldt County. Due to the south-facing view, the lighthouse and the dwelling had ample sun and warmth in the wintertime. The original Cape Cod dwelling of 1871 was added on to in 1898 after the completion of the bell house. Early on, the keepers' supplies arrived by lighthouse tender, and the sight of the *Madrono* and the *Sequoia* steaming the cove was a welcome one. Supplies were landed on the beach between Trinidad Head and the mainland and hauled by wagon up the windy road to the house. Fred Harrington ordered a lot of his grocery supplies from San Francisco, where they would load it on the government pier and transport it up to Trinidad. If one saw a flag flying on the mast, it meant that the lighthouse inspector was on the ship. Everyone would scramble, ensuring all uniforms were pressed, and a horse and wagon were sent down to the beach to bring the inspector up to the lighthouse. (Courtesy of Trinidad Museum Society.)

Jeremiah Kiler, a native of New York, was the Trinidad Head Lighthouse keeper from 1871 until his death in 1888. When he and his wife, Sarah, arrived from Vermont, they were in their mid-50s. They had one son, Fred, who was already in his 20s by the time the pair arrived at the small town of Trinidad and traveled up the wagon road to the short 25-foot lighthouse that stood on the 200-foot cliff face of Trinidad Head. Kiler lit the lamp on December 1, and his wife, Sarah, assisted him in his duties. Fred Harrington succeeded Kiler in 1888, and nearly 100 years later, the grandchildren of both lighthouse keepers, Edith Kiler and Milton Hunter, married one another. Edith was the daughter of Fred Kiler, Sarah and Jeremiah's only son. Milton was the son of Maude, Fred Harrington's only daughter. The marriage between lighthouse keepers and their families was extremely common as they shared a familiar past and the intimate community connection. (Courtesy of Trinidad Museum Society.)

Upon the completion of the Trinidad Head Lighthouse in 1871, a notice to mariners was published as a safety announcement with descriptions of the light, dwelling, and the lighthouse. The notice read, "A revolving red light of the fourth order, of the system of Fresnel will be exhibited for the first time on the evening of December 1st, 1871, and on every evening thereafter, from the tower recently erected on the southern slope of Trinidad Head. The apparatus is arranged to produce: a red flash of 5 seconds and a partial eclipse of 5 seconds, and a total eclipse every 45 seconds. The tower is of brick, painted white except the dome and railing, which are red. The keeper's dwelling is a two-story wooden building painted white and is 50 yards to the N.E. of the tower. The usual out-houses are to the rear of the dwelling." Here, Capt. Jeremiah Kiler stands along the railing. (Courtesy of Trinidad Museum Society.)

Malcolm Cady was born in 1876 in Petrolia to Eliza Hunter, sister of Paschal Hunter, Punta Gorda's first lighthouse keeper. Cady began his lighthouse career in 1904 at Point Arena Lighthouse, transferred to the new Point Loma Lighthouse as first assistant, and ultimately moved to Trinidad Head in 1930, retiring from his nearly 40-year career as principal keeper in 1940. Water at Trinidad Head had been a consistent issue since the lighthouse was built. Initially, water was collected in tanks from the roof run-off, and fresh water had to be brought in from town for cooking and drinking during the summer. In the 1930s, it was Cady who found a sustainable source of water, a spring on the east side of the head. It was plumbed to the dwellings. Eventually, a water line was connected to the city of Trinidad in the 1960s. During Cady's tenure, he was privy to the construction of a whaling station in the wharf in 1920. (Courtesy of Boyle Collection, Humboldt State University.)

By 1942, the oil lamp was electrified, and the bell was replaced in 1947 with compressed air horns. The Coast Guard razed the Colonial lighthouse keeper dwellings in the late 1960s and replaced them with barracks. It was a new era, not only for the Trinidad Head Lighthouse but also for the entire United States. Gone were the days of the sole lighthouse keeper like Fred Harrington. In 1985, Harrington's grandson Ralph Hunter described a memory where his grandfather Fred, on a nightly basis, would sit just inside the window of his house, rocking in his chair, smoking his pipe, and watching the flash, which showed a little bit of an orange glow, every 45 seconds, flashing and illuminating the coast. Hunter was comforted by the fact that his grandfather was making a difference by keeping the harbors and mariners safe for the night. (Courtesy of Library of Congress.)

Bibliography

Clark, D.J. "The Humboldt Harbor Lighthouse." *Humboldt Historian*. Winter 2011: 10–21.

Evans, B. "The Punta Gorda Light." *Humboldt Historian*. Spring 2015: 20–21.

House, Freeman, and Ray Raphael. *Two Peoples, One Place*. Eureka, CA: Humboldt County Historical Society, 2011.

Hunter, R. Personal interview by Burch Calkins. Trinidad, CA, 1985.

Mattson, Jan Robert. *California Lighthouse Keepers*. Cardiff, CA: Goat Rock Publications, 2016.

Shanks, Ralph, and Janetta Shanks. *Lighthouses and Lifeboats on the Redwood Coast*. San Anselmo, CA: Costano Books, 1978.

Shepherd, M. *The Sea Captain's Odyssey: A Biography of Captain H.H. Buhne*. Walnut Creek, CA: Georgie Press, 2011.

About the Organization

The Trinidad Museum Society, incorporated in 1983 and located in an 1899 Victorian Italianate bungalow called the Sangster-Watkins-Underwood home at 400 Janis Court, highlights the cultural and natural history of Trinidad. Permanent exhibits include the 1940s lighthouse lens from the 1871 Trinidad Head Lighthouse, a redwood Yurok dugout canoe, a late-1800s A.W. Ericson printing press, an exhibit on the 1775 Spanish voyage of Bruno Hezeta and Juan Francisco de la Bodega y Quadra when Trinidad was claimed for King Carlos III, and a native plant garden. Rotating exhibits of historic photographs, Native American history, fungi, flowers, geology, and economic and social history are shown in five rooms in the restored home. The Trinidad Museum, as one of the partners of the California Coastal National Monument–Bureau of Land Management, hosts regular first Saturday tours of the Trinidad Head Lighthouse. Visit the Trinidad Museum Society's website at www.trinidadmuseum.org.